Edexcel GCSE

History B
Schools History Project
Germany 1918–1945

Author:

Steve Waugh

Series Editor:

Angela Leonard

Updated for the
2013 specifications by:

Jane Shuter

ALWAYS LEARNING   **PEARSON**

Published by Pearson Education Limited, Edinburgh Gate, Harlow, Essex, CM20 2JE.

www.pearsonschoolsandfecolleges.co.uk

Copies of official specifications for all Edexcel qualifications may be found on the Edexcel website: www.edexcel.com

Text © Pearson Education Limited 2013
Typeset and illustrated by HL Studios, Witney, Oxford
Original illustrations © Pearson Education Limited 2009
Cover photo/illustration © *Front:* **akg-images Ltd**

The rights of Steve Waugh and Jane Shuter to be identified as authors of this work have been asserted by them in accordance with the Copyright, Designs and Patents Act 1988.

First published 2013

16 15
10 9 8 7 6 5 4 3 2

British Library Cataloguing in Publication Data
A catalogue record for this book is available from the British Library

ISBN 978 1 446906 83 5

Printed by Neografia

Acknowledgements
The author and publisher would like to thank the following individuals and organisations for permission to reproduce photographs:
(Key: b-bottom; c-centre; l-left; r-right; t-top)

akg-images Ltd: 6b, 22, 27, 28, 35, 44t, 47, 64br, 85, 98, Collection Archiv f.Kunst & Geschichte 95, Ullstein Bild 67; **Alamy Images:** INTERFOTO Pressbildagentur 44c, 61tr, Mary Evans Picture Library 94, Photos 12, 71, The Print Collector / Art Media 21; **Bridgeman Art Library Ltd:** Deutsches Historiches Museum, Berlin, Germany / DHM Arne Psille 73, Kungstgewerbe Museum, Zurichm Switzerland / Archives Charmet 15, Laket Museum, Essen, Germany / Archives Charmet 51, Private Collection / Archives Charmet 70c, 88, Private Collection / Peter Newark Military Pictures 79, Private Collection / Peter Newark Pictures 25, 55; **Bundesarchiv (Federal Archives):** 60; **Corbis:** Austrian Archives 53, Bettmann 39l, 39r, Stapleton Collection 107; **David King Collection:** 57; **FotoLibra:** 6c, 12, 23, 70b, 86, 102; **Getty Images:** Dmitri Kessel / Time Life Pictures 64cr, Hulton Archive 16, Popperfoto 61tl; **iStockphoto:** Stockphoto4u 114; **Bildarchiv Preussischer Kulturbesitz:** 7, 17, 18, 56, 72, 74t; **Mary Evans Picture Library:** 9, 74b, Weimar Library 82; **Photoshot Holdings Limited:** 44b, 59t, 64cl, 66, UPPA 20, 50-51; **Randall Bytwerk:** 70t, 77; **Rex Features:** 6t, Roger-Viollet 97; **The Wiener Library:** 80; **TopFoto:** 45, Roger-Viollet 33, Topham PicturePoint 64c, Ullstein Bild 59b, 64bl, 90, 92

All other images © Pearson Education

We are grateful to the following for permission to reproduce copyright material:

Source C on page 10 from *Modern Germany: Society, Economy and Politics in the Twentieth Century Cambridge University Press; 2 edition (27 Nov 1987) ISBN-13: 978-0521347488* (V. R. Berghahn 1987); Source B on page 16 and Source D on page 17 from *Mein Kampf by Adolph Hitler*, published by Hutchinson. Reprinted by permission of The Random House Group Limited, translated by Ralph Manheim. Copyright (c) 1943, renewed 1971 by Houghton Mifflin Harcourt Publishing Company. Reprinted by permission of Houghton Mifflin Harcourt Publishing Company. All rights reserved; Source F on page 51 from *Steven Waugh, Essential Modern World History*, published by Nelson Thornes in 2001; Source D on page 58 from *Germany 1918-1945 (Oxford History for GCSE) ISBN-13: 978-0199132775*, OUP Oxford (J A Cloake) 2000 by kind permission of The Oxford University Press; Source E on page 58 from *Weimar and Nazi Germany: Weimar and Nazi Germany ISBN-13: 978-0719573439 p.204*, Hodder Education (John Hite, Chris Hinton) 2000; Source B on page 60 from *Mein Kampf by Adolph Hitler*, published by Hutchinson. Reprinted by permission of The Random House Group Limited, translated by Ralph Manheim. Copyright (c) 1943, renewed 1971 by Houghton Mifflin Harcourt Publishing Company. Reprinted by permission of Houghton Mifflin Harcourt Publishing Company. All rights reserved; Source E on page 61 from *Germany 1918-1945 Oxford History for GCSE ISBN 0199132771*, The Oxford University Press (J A Cloake 1997) by kind permission of The Oxford University Press; Source F on page 75 from *Weimar and Nazi Germany: Weimar and Nazi Germany (SHP Advanced History Core Texts) ISBN-13: 978-0719573439*, Hodder Education (Chris Hinton John Hite) 2000; Source F on page 78 from *A Boy in Your Situation ISBN-13: 978-0233982793* Scholastic (Charles Hannam) 13 Oct 1988 reprinted with permission from Scholastic Children's Books (UK); Source A on page 82 from *Nazism 1919-1945: A Documentary Reader, Vol IV The German Home Front in World War II, ISBN 0 85989* Univ. of Exeter Press (Jeremy Noakes) 1998 with kind permission of Liverpool University Press; Source A on page 91 from *Heinemann Advanced History: Germany 1919-45 ISBN-13: 978-0435327217* Heinemann (Martin Collier, Philip Pedley 2001), Pearson Education Ltd; Source B on page 91 from *Hitler and Germany (Cambridge Topics in History) ISBN-13: 978-0521376297*, Cambridge University Press (William Simpson) 1991; Source B on page 92 and Source C on page 93 from *War Wives* © Copyright Colin and Eileen Townsend 1989. Reproduced by permission of Sheil Land Associates Ltd; Extract on page 105 from *Germany 1918-1945 (Oxford History for GCSE) ISBN-13: 978-0199132775* J A Cloake, OUP Oxford (2000)

Every effort has been made to contact copyright holders of material reproduced in this book. Any omissions will be rectified in subsequent printings if notice is given to the publishers.

Contents

A note from the publisher

In order to ensure that this student book offers high-quality support for the associated Edexcel qualification, it has been through a review process by the awarding organisation to confirm that it fully covers the teaching and learning content of the specification or part of a specification at which it is aimed, and demonstrates an appropriate balance between the development of subject skills, knowledge and understanding, in addition to preparation for assessment.

While the publishers have made every attempt to ensure that advice on the qualification and its assessment is accurate, the official specification and associated assessment guidance materials are the only authoritative source of information and should always be referred to for definitive guidance.

Edexcel examiners have not contributed to any updated sections in this resource relevant to examination papers for which they have responsibility.

No material from an endorsed student book will be used verbatim in any assessment set by Edexcel.

Endorsement of a student book does not mean that the student book is required to achieve this Edexcel qualification, nor does it mean that it is the only suitable material available to support the qualification, and any resource lists produced by the awarding organisation shall include this and other appropriate resources.

Websites

There are links to relevant websites in this book. In order to ensure that the links are up to date, that the links work, and that the sites are not inadvertently linked to sites that could be considered offensive, we have made the links available on the Pearson website at www.pearsonhotlinks.co.uk. When you access the site, the express code is 4448P.

Disclaimer

This Edexcel publication offers high-quality support for the delivery of Edexcel qualifications. Edexcel endorsement does not mean that this material is essential to achieve any Edexcel qualification, nor does it mean that this is the only suitable material available to support any Edexcel qualification. No endorsed material will be used verbatim in setting any Edexcel examination and any resource lists produced by Edexcel shall include this and other appropriate texts.

Copies of official specifications for all Edexcel qualifications may be found on the Edexcel website – www.edexcel.com.

Welcome to this Edexcel GCSE History B: Schools History Project Resource

Option 2C: Life in Germany 1918–1945

These resources are appropriate for GCSE History students on the linear GCSE course certificated from 2015. This course has a focus on change and development through studies of societies in depth and of key themes over time. Packed with exam tips and activities, the book includes lots of engaging features to enthuse students and provide the range of support needed to make teaching and learning a success for all ability levels.

How to use this book

Edexcel GCSE History B: Schools History Project Life in Germany 1918–1945 is divided into the three sections of the specification:

- Weimar Germany and the rise of the Nazi Party
- The Government of the Third Reich to 1945
- The Social impact of the Nazi state to 1945.

Features of this book

Learning outcomes structure learning at the start of each topic.

FASCINATING FACTS give learning extra depth.

Key words are highlighted and defined for easy reference.

A topic **Summary** captures the main learning points.

Activities provide stimulating tasks for the classroom and homework.

A dedicated suite of revision resources. We've broken down the six stages of revision to ensure that you are prepared every step of the way.

Tips and advice on how to plan your revision effectively.

A checklist of things you should know, revision activities and practice exam questions at the end of each section plus additional exam practice at the end of the book.

Last-minute advice for just before the exam.

An overview of what you will have to do in the exam, plus a chance to see what a real exam paper will look like.

What do you do after your exam? This section contains information on how to get your results and answers to frequently asked questions on what to do next.

These features help you to understand how to improve, with guidance on answering exam-style questions, tips on how to remember important concepts and how to avoid common pitfalls.

There are four different types of Exam Zone features throughout this book:

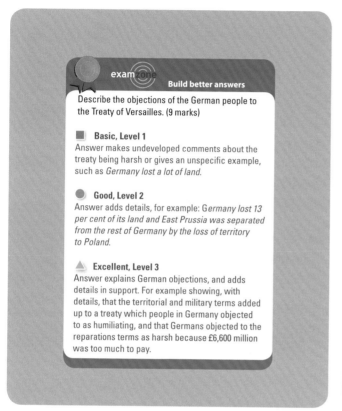

Build better answers give you an opportunity to answer exam-style questions. They include tips for what a basic ■ good ● and excellent ▲ answer will contain.

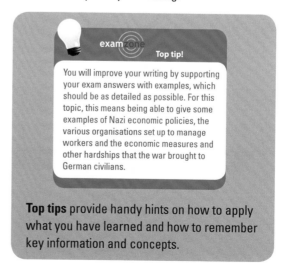

The KnowZone Build better answers pages at the end of each section include an exam-style question with a student answer, comments and an improved answer so that you can see how to improve your writing.

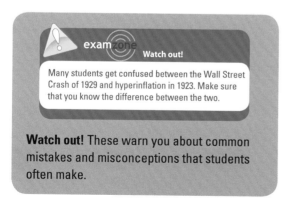

Watch out! These warn you about common mistakes and misconceptions that students often make.

Top tips provide handy hints on how to apply what you have learned and how to remember key information and concepts.

Weimar Germany and the rise of the Nazi Party

Introduction

German defeat in the First World War brought about the downfall of the German ruler, Kaiser William II, in 1918. He was replaced by a republic, which was set up in 1919, in the south German town of Weimar.

The Weimar Republic enjoyed mixed fortunes. It was very unpopular in its early years, 1919–1923, mainly because it signed the hated Treaty of Versailles, but also because of hyperinflation. However, it recovered in the years 1923–1929, mainly due to the work of Gustav Stresemann, only to become unpopular again in the years after 1929 as a result of the Great Depression.

The rise of the Nazi Party, led from 1921 by Adolf Hitler, was closely linked to the fortunes of the Weimar Republic. When the Republic was popular, in the years 1924–1929, the Nazis had little support. However, as the Republic became more and more unpopular after 1929, because of high unemployment, support for Hitler and the Nazis increased.

German children play with bundles of real money.

This cartoon is about the Treaty of Versailles.

Aims and outcomes

By the end of this section, you should be able to understand, describe and explain...

- the fortunes of the Weimar Republic in the years 1919–1932
- the key features of the Nazi Party, 1919–1928
- the reasons for increased support for the Nazi Party in the years 1929–1932.

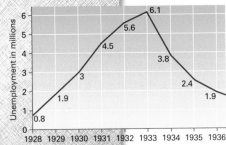

The effects of the Wall Street Crash on unemployment.

1918	1919	1920	1921	1923	1924	1925
Kaiser abdicates and Germany signs the armistice.	Weimar Republic is set up and signs the Treaty of Versailles. Spartacist uprising.	Nazi Party set up and the Kapp *Putsch*.	Hitler becomes leader of the Nazi Party.	French occupation of the Ruhr, hyperinflation and the Munich *Putsch*.	Hitler spends nine months in prison. The Dawes Plan is signed.	Germany signs the Locarno Treaties.

A 1932 Nazi election poster: 'Women! Millions of men without work. Millions of children without a future. Save the German family. Vote Adolf Hitler!'

Activities

1 Work in pairs, sitting back-to-back:

   a) Describe the Nazi poster on this page to your partner, who will make a sketch based on your description (rather than from what they can recall from the textbook).

   b) Both of you compare your partner's version of the poster with the original.

   c) How accurate is the sketch compared to the original?

2 Why do you think this poster encouraged German voters to support Hitler and the Nazi Party?

3 What Nazi ideas can you identify from the poster?

FASCINATING FACT

Adolf Hitler, who became ruler of Germany in the 1930s and arguably the most powerful leader in the world, spent several years in his late teens and early twenties as a down-and-out in Vienna.

1926 Germany joins the League of Nations.

1928 Nazis win only twelve seats in the *Reichstag*.

1929 Death of Stresemann. Wall Street Crash.

1930 Nazis win 107 seats in the *Reichstag*.

1932 Unemployment reaches 6 million. Nazis win 230 seats and become the largest Party in the *Reichstag*.

1.1 The early years of the Weimar Republic, 1918-1923

Learning outcomes

By the end of this topic you should be able to:

- understand the early problems of the Weimar Republic
- explain the reasons for early opposition to the Weimar Republic
- describe how successful the Weimar Republic was in dealing with these problems and the opposition it encountered.

Activities

Look at the storyboard.

1 What reasons are suggested for the early unpopularity of the Weimar Republic?

2 Which groups wanted to overthrow the Republic?

Getting an overview

In November 1918 there was a revolution in Germany due to defeat in the First World War. Kaiser William II was forced to abdicate and was replaced by a republic.

The Weimar Republic was set up in 1919. The Republic was ruled by a President, a Chancellor and parliament, but it had too many political parties, which led to it being ruled by weak governments.

The Republic was unpopular because it was forced to sign the Treaty of Versailles, which many Germans disagreed with.

There were two attempts to overthrow the Republic in the years 1919–1922. One was by communists known as the Spartacists, and the other by members of the army – in the Kapp *Putsch*.

Hitler hated the Treaty of Versailles and the new Republic and was determined to destroy them both. He believed that the Republic had betrayed the German army and the German people.

By 1922 Hitler had set up the Nazi Party, which had its own private army, known as the Brownshirts, and its own emblem, the *swastika*. Hitler wanted to overthrow the Republic by force.

Armistice: Ceasefire

Coalition: A government by two or more political parties

Constitution: System of rules by which a country is governed

Judiciary: Judges

Kaiser: German title for Emperor

Orator: A fluent and effective public speaker

Putsch: An uprising, an attempt to overthrow the government

Reichstag: Parliament

Reparations: Compensation for war damages, paid by a defeated state

Spartacists: The name of the German Communist Party

The formation of the Weimar Republic

Why was there a revolution in Germany in November 1918?

The revolution in November 1918 was due to Germany's defeat in the First World War. Germany had gone to war in 1914 against France, Britain and Russia, confident of an early victory. Although generally successful in the east against Russia, the German armed forces were dragged into a long drawn-out conflict with France and Britain on the Western Front. The entry of the United States in 1917 against Germany tipped the balance of the conflict and by early November 1918 German armies were in retreat, and Germany itself was threatened with occupation.

Furthermore, the war had brought terrible hardships to the German people. The British navy had blockaded the German coastline throughout the war, preventing the import of much-needed supplies of raw materials and food. By 1918 there were serious food shortages and increasing opposition to the war. In addition, a serious flu epidemic killed many German people.

Source A: A cartoon drawn in 1918. The cartoon shows Kaiser William II in the centre with figures on either side, representing war on the left and starvation on the right.

Source B: From a telephone call made by Gustav Noske, one of the leaders of the Social Democrats.

> '… The situation is almost hopeless. General chaos is imminent and power is slipping more and more into the hands of revolutionary sailors.'

The revolution originated from sailors in the German navy in the port of Kiel. At the end of October 1918, they refused to set out to fight the British navy. Instead they marched to Berlin where they were joined by many discontented civilians, all demanding the abdication of **Kaiser** William II, who was blamed for Germany's defeat. On 9 November, the *Kaiser* abdicated and went to live in exile in Holland. On the following day, a republic was set up under its new President, Friedrich Ebert, who was the leader of the Social Democratic Party. Finally, on 11 November, the new republic agreed to an **armistice**.

What was the 'stab in the back' theory?

The 'stab in the back' theory was the belief, put forward by leading members of the German army, and later supported by Hitler and the Nazis, that the German army had been on the verge of winning the war when they were betrayed by the politicians of the new republic, who agreed to the armistice. Although untrue, the theory was believed by many Germans, who refused to accept that Germany had been defeated. This meant that the Republic was unpopular with many from the start.

How was the Weimar Republic set up?

Germany was a federation of eighteen states, each with its own parliament, police and laws. In January 1919, elections took place for a new parliament. This new parliament met in the south German town of Weimar, because of the fighting that was taking place in Berlin between the **Spartacists** and the *Freikorps* (see page 15). The parliament made two important decisions. First of all, it elected Ebert as President. Secondly, it set up a new **constitution** for the new Germany.

Activities

1 What is the message of the cartoonist in Source A?

2 Was this unpopularity justified?

What were the strengths and weaknesses of the new constitution?

The President
Elected every seven years. Had the power to appoint the Chancellor. Article 48 said that in an emergency the president could make laws without going to the Reichstag.

The Chancellor
Appointed by the President and equivalent of the British Prime Minister. Had to have the support of the majority of the Reichstag.

The Reichstag
Equivalent of the House of Commons. Power to pass or reject changes in the law. Elected by proportional representation every four years.

The German people
All adults over the age of twenty could vote for the President and the Reichstag. Had equal rights including the right of free speech, to travel freely, to hold political meetings and freedom of religious belief.

Source C: From a history of Germany 1918–1945, written in 1945.

'The new constitution had many strengths. All Germans had equal rights, including the right to vote. A strong President was necessary to keep control over the government and to protect the country in a crisis. The states had their own traditions and kept their own governments and some control over their own affairs.'

Proportional representation

Proportional representation was one of the strengths of the new constitution, but one of its weaknesses at the same time. Positively, it made sure that all parties were given a fair share of the seats in the **Reichstag** but, on the other hand, it seriously weakened the government of the new republic.

It led to many, often small, parties, including extremist groups such as the Nazis.

↓

No one party was large enough to secure a majority in the Reichstag.

↓

Several parties often had to join together to form a **coalition** government.

↓

These coalition governments were often weak and short lived.

Source D: The results of the elections of 1920 for the Reichstag.

Party	Percentage of votes	Number of seats
Social Democrats (SPD)	22	102
Centre (Zentrum)	13.6	64
Liberal Progressives (DDP)	8.3	39
Conservatives (DNVP)	15.1	71
Independent Socialists (USPD)	19.7	84
National Liberals (DVP)	13.9	65
Communists (KPD)	2.1	4

The constitution had several other weaknesses. The Republic had many enemies and the new constitution gave opposition groups the freedom to criticise and even attack the new government. Moreover, the constitution made no attempt to change traditional institutions, such as the army and **judiciary**, who had supported the *Kaiser* and did not welcome the new republic. This undermined the Republic from the outset. Additionally, the President had too much power, most especially with the use of Article 48 (see page 39) in a time of emergency.

Activities

3 What does Source D suggest about proportional representation?

4 Working in pairs, make a copy of the following grid to use for your answers. You need to research the strengths to complete the left-hand column, while your partner researches the weaknesses to complete the right-hand column.

'The Weimar constitution had more strengths than weaknesses.' From the evidence, how far do you agree or disagree with this view?

Strengths of constitution	Weaknesses of constitution

Together, look at the conclusion suggested by your research.

Each of you should then decide how much you agree or disagree with this conclusion. Explain why.

What were the main terms of the Treaty of Versailles?

In June 1919, Germany was forced by the victorious countries to sign the Treaty of Versailles (having been excluded from the talks).

Territorial terms
- Alsace-Lorraine was returned to France.
- West Prussia, Upper Silesia and Posen were given to Poland.
- Eupen and Malmédy lost to Belgium.
- Danzig was taken over by the League of Nations as a free city.
- Memel was taken over by the League and eventually given to Lithuania in 1923.
- The Saarland was taken over by the League of Nations for 15 years.
- Germany also lost all of its overseas colonies. They were run by the victorious powers on behalf of the League of Nations.

■ Territory lost by Germany in the Treaty

■ Demilitarised land

TERMS OF TREATY OF VERSAILLES

Reparations
The War Guilt Clause meant that the victorious powers could demand compensation from Germany for the damage caused by the war. This was known as **reparations**. In 1921, the Reparations Commission fixed the sum at £6,600 million, which had to be paid in annual instalments.

War Guilt
Article 231 of the Treaty said that Germany was to blame for causing the war. This was the term that the Germans most resented. They believed that other countries had caused the war and that Germany went to war in self-defence.

Military terms
- Germany was not allowed military aircraft or submarines.
- The navy was reduced to six battleships and 15,000 sailors.
- The army was reduced to 100,000.
- The Rhineland area was demilitarised – this meant no German armed forces in the area. Allied troops to occupy the area for fifteen years.

Activities

5 What is meant by the following terms?
   a) Reparations
   b) War Guilt
   c) Demilitarisation of the Rhineland.

6 Study the map of the territorial terms above. Identify two things you can learn from the map about these terms.

7 Which of the four main parts of the Treaty of Versailles punished Germany the most?

In order to look at this, make a copy of the following circle diagram. Then put each of the four main parts of the Treaty in each of the four circles, placing them in order from the worst (from the German point of view) in the centre to the least on the outside circle.

Why was there opposition in Germany to the Versailles Treaty?

Most Germans believed that although they would have to pay a price for losing the war, the terms would be reasonable. After all, their revolution had removed the *Kaiser*, who had been mainly responsible for the war. He had been replaced by a democratically elected government, which believed that the Allies (Britain, France and the United States) would be sympathetic and not overly harsh. Moreover, the US President, Woodrow Wilson, had promised that it would be a fair treaty based on his 'Fourteen Points'.

However, the French and British were determined to make sure that Germany paid the price of war and could not become a threat again. The majority of Germans were shocked at the severity of the terms of the Treaty. There was a blaze of protest in the German press and mob violence, especially in Berlin and Hamburg.

The German government had no choice but to accept the terms. Refusal would have precipitated an Allied occupation of Germany. They were, however, blamed by many Germans, most especially Hitler and the Nazis, for the harsh peace terms. The Allies had seriously undermined the position of the new republic.

The German people had many objections to the Treaty. They had not been invited to the peace conference and they described the Treaty as a *diktat* (or dictated peace), imposed without any opportunity for negotiation or compromise. The military terms threatened to destroy the country's status as a great power and leave Germany vulnerable to attack from neighbours. It left many in the armed forces out of work and angry.

Possibly more humiliating was the occupation of the Rhineland by Allied troops.

Source E: From a German First World War soldier.

'All of a sudden, we are confronted with what the bulk of the Germans considered an entirely unjust treaty. So resistance against this Treaty was enormous. I think that the strongest resistance concerned the territorial concessions in the East. Nobody was willing to concede that much territory to the new Polish State. Nobody was willing to accept willingly the system of reparations.'

Source F: A cartoon from a German magazine in July 1919. Clemenceau, the French President, is shown as a vampire. The person on the bed represents Germany.

Activities

8   Imagine you are the editor of a German newspaper. Devise a suitable caption for Source F.

9   Why was there strong opposition to the Treaty from many Germans?

Write a brief essay answering this question. You may use the following in your answer together with any other information of your own:

- Reparations
- Military terms
- Territorial terms.

10 Do you agree with the view given in Source G that the 'victors shifted their financial burdens on to the defeated'?

11 Working in pairs, draw a table with two column headings: 'Opposition justified' and 'Opposition not justified'. Complete your table with evidence for each side of the argument.

12 Do you believe that German opposition to the Treaty of Versailles was justified? Explain your conclusion.

Source G: The views of John Maynard Keynes.

'The future life of Europe was not the concern of the Allied leaders, its economy was not their anxiety. Their concerns, good and bad alike, related to frontiers and nationalities, to the future weakening of a strong and dangerous enemy, to revenge. The victors shifted their unbearable financial burdens onto the shoulders of the defeated.'

How justified was this opposition?

There has been much discussion and much debate about the Treaty of Versailles, both at the time and later. There were several critics of the Treaty, most notably the famous British economist John Maynard Keynes, who thought that the German opposition to the Treaty was justified. Indeed, he resigned from the British delegation to Versailles in protest at the peace terms. See Source G.

examzone
Build better answers

Describe the objections of the German people to the Treaty of Versailles. (9 marks)

◼ **Basic, Level 1**
Answer makes undeveloped comments about the treaty being harsh or gives an unspecific example, such as *Germany lost a lot of land.*

● **Good, Level 2**
Answer adds details, for example: G*ermany lost 13 per cent of its land and East Prussia was separated from the rest of Germany by the loss of territory to Poland.*

▲ **Excellent, Level 3**
Answer explains German objections, and adds details in support. For example showing, with details, that the territorial and military terms added up to a treaty which people in Germany objected to as humiliating, and that Germans objected to the reparations terms as harsh because £6,600 million was too much to pay.

The territorial terms seemed to rob Germany of key industrial areas, such as the iron and steel of Alsace-Lorraine and the coalfields of the Saar, as well as raw materials from ex-colonies in Africa and the Far East. The loss of territory to Poland created what became known as the 'Polish Corridor', an area that separated part of Germany, East Prussia, from the rest of Germany. Germany lost 13 per cent of its land. This would have a severe impact on Germany's economy.

The War Guilt clause was the one the Germans resented most. To them the war had been one of self-defence. At the very least, from their point of view, other nations such as Russia, France and Britain ought to accept some responsibility for the outbreak of war in 1914. Moreover, Germany had suffered badly as a result of the war and was in no position to make annual **reparation** payments, having lost around 10 per cent of its industry and 15 per cent of its agricultural land.

Opposition to the Weimar Republic

The Weimar Republic was not popular with many Germans in the years 1919–1922. This was partly due to weaknesses in the new constitution, being forced to sign the Treaty of Versailles and the 'stab in the back' theory. Moreover, most Germans were not used to democracy and some wanted the return of the *Kaiser*. The diagram shows the three main groups that threatened the Weimar Republic.

The Spartacist uprising
This was the name of the German Communist party, which was led by Rosa Luxemburg and Karl Liebknecht. They wanted to overthrow the Republic and set up a communist government. Their attempt to seize power in January 1919 was unsuccessful when the Republic called upon the *Freikorps*, volunteer ex servicemen, who shot the two leaders for 'resisting arrest'.

The Kapp *Putsch*
This was an attempt by the *Freikorps* to overthrow the Weimar Republic in March 1920, led by Dr Kapp, a strong opponent of the Republic and the Treaty of Versailles. The *Freikorps* seized Berlin and forced the government to flee. The ***putsch*** was defeated by a workers' general strike.

The Nazis
Hitler believed in the 'stab in the back' theory and strongly opposed the Treaty of Versailles. He was determined to overthrow the Weimar Republic. By 1921 he had his own party, the Nazis, which, within two years, had attracted a number of supporters as well as its own private army, known as the stormtroopers or Brownshirts.

Activities

1 Make a copy of the following table and list three examples of similarities and differences between the Spartacist uprising and the Kapp *Putsch*. Lightly shade the similarities and leave the differences white. One example has been done for you.

	Spartacist uprising	Kapp *Putsch*
1	Wanted to overthrow the Weimar Republic	Wanted to overthrow the Weimar Republic
2		
3		

Who were the Spartacists?

The Spartacist League (named after a famous gladiator called Spartacus who led a revolt in ancient Rome) were communists inspired by the success of the communist takeover in Russia in 1917. They did not believe that Ebert and the Social Democrats would serve the interests of the German working people. They were led by Rosa Luxemburg (known as 'Red Rosa'), a brilliant speaker and writer, and Karl Liebknecht.

Source A: A Spartacist poster. The three heads represent militarism, capitalism and the landowners.

Extreme members of the Spartacists staged an uprising in Berlin on 5 January 1919. They seized the headquarters of the government's newspaper and telegraph bureau and tried to organise a general strike. However, it was badly organised and received little support from the people of Berlin.

The day after the uprising, Ebert, with the support of the army leaders, used a volunteer force of 4,000 ex-soldiers known as the *Freikorps* (Free Corps). They were hard men who hated the communists and liked to fight. By 15 January the Spartacists were crushed. Their two leaders were arrested and, during transportation to prison, were shot by two members of the *Freikorps* while apparently 'resisting arrest'. Their murder genuinely shocked President Ebert.

The Spartacists were important for two main reasons:

- Their uprising highlighted the instability of the Weimar Republic. A socialist, left-wing government had been attacked by an even more left-wing group.

- The uprising left the new republic dependent on the support of the army, which had been needed to crush the revolt. In return for this support, the Republic promised not to change the army leadership.

Activities

2 What is the message being put across by the Spartacists in Source A?

3 Describe the ways in which the Spartacists threatened the new republic.

What was the Kapp *Putsch*?

The *Freikorps* hated the Treaty of Versailles and the Weimar Republic for signing it. When the Treaty came into effect on 1 January 1920, the government began to reduce the size of their army to 100,000. This cut included disbanding the *Freikorps*.

The *Freikorps* were furious and in March 1920, led by Dr Wolfgang Kapp, an extreme nationalist, they attempted to take power in Berlin. Kapp set up a new government in Berlin. The Weimar government fled to Dresden but, before leaving Berlin, called upon the trade unions of Berlin to organise a general strike in order to paralyse the city, cutting off gas, electricity, food and coal supplies and bringing industry to a halt. However, the vast majority of the army refused to move against Kapp and his 5,000 followers.

Nonetheless, Kapp found he could not rule Germany because of the chaos caused by the general strike. He had to abandon his plans and flee to Sweden.

The Kapp *Putsch* showed that the Republic had gained much support from the workers of Berlin. On the other hand, it revealed the lack of support from the army who sympathised with the aims of the *Putsch*.

Activities

4 Why do you think the army mostly refused to move against Kapp and his followers?

5 Which was the more serious threat to the Republic – the Spartacist uprising or the Kapp *Putsch*? Give your reasons.

Who was Adolf Hitler?

Munich

In May 1913 Hitler moved to Munich, partly because of the prominence of Jews in Vienna, but mainly to avoid possible arrest for failure to register for military service in the Austrian army between 1909 and 1912.

Birth

Hitler was born in 1889 in the village of Braunau, in Austria. His father, who he disliked, was a customs official and died when Adolf was 13. His mother, who he worshipped, died when he was 18.

Education

He spent five years at primary school followed by four years at middle school. He did not do well at school and described his teachers as *'absolute tyrants. They had no sympathy with youth. Their one object was to stuff our brains and turn us into educated apes'*. He left school with no qualifications.

**Adolf Hitler.
This is your life!**

Soldier

When the First World War broke out, Hitler enthusiastically volunteered to serve in the German army. Later he wrote *'I am not ashamed even today to say that, overwhelmed by impassioned enthusiasm, I had fallen on my knees and thanked God'*. He was a good soldier who won medals for bravery. His officers noticed that he was a very effective speaker and gave him the job of countering enemy propaganda.

Vienna

Hitler was determined to be an artist. However, his hopes were dashed when, in 1907, he failed the entrance exam to the Vienna Academy of Fine Arts. He soon ran out of money and was forced to live in a hostel for the homeless, living no better than a down-and-out. He raised some money by painting and selling postcards. It was in Vienna that he first developed his hatred for the Jews as well as his belief in nationalism. In February 1914 he returned to Vienna but was found unfit for the army.

Source B: From Hitler's autobiography *Mein Kampf*, written in 1925.

'I was orphaned at the age of eighteen and was forced to earn my living as a simple worker. I became a labourer on a building site and during the next two years, did every type of casual job. With great effort I was able to teach myself to paint in my spare time. I earned a small living by this work. By the age of 21 I had become an architectural draughtsman and painter and was completely independent.'

Source C: Hitler as a soldier in 1917.

Activities

6 Study Source B. Is this a true account of Hitler's life in Vienna? Why do you think he wrote this account?

7 Make a copy of the following table and complete it with information about Hitler's early life.

Positive achievements	Negative experiences

16

How did Hitler become the leader of the Nazis?

In 1918 Hitler was badly gassed and was in hospital when the armistice was signed in November 1918. Source D tells how he reacted when he heard of Germany's surrender.

Source D: From *Mein Kampf.*

> 'It became impossible for me to sit still one minute more. I tottered and groped my way back to my dormitory, threw myself on my bunk, and dug my burning head into my blanket and pillow and sobbed.'

Germany's defeat in 1918 left Hitler extremely bitter and, like many other Germans, he needed a scapegoat, someone to blame for the defeat. In the same way as many other soldiers, he blamed Germany's defeat on the communists and Jews, who he felt had stabbed the German army in the back. After the war, he returned to Munich.

However, he was still employed by the army to check up on any extremist groups in Munich. In September 1919 Hitler was sent to a meeting of a small extremist group known as the German Workers' Party, which had been set up earlier in the year by Anton Drexler. It only had six committee members. Within a week, he had joined and became committee member number seven. This was partly because he was impressed with the Party's ideas. Drexler wanted to appeal to the working classes but also was a strong nationalist who opposed the Treaty of Versailles. Moreover, Hitler realised he had more chance of becoming leader of a small group rather than one of the bigger, mainstream parties.

In February 1920 he was put in charge of propaganda. The Party later bought control of a newspaper, *The Observer.* On 24 February 1920 he advertised a meeting. Almost 2,000 people attended. At this meeting, Hitler announced the Party's new name: the National Socialist German Workers' Party (NSDAP) or Nazis. He also announced his Twenty-Five Point programme.

Hitler showed a real talent for public speaking and attracted an increasing number of followers to the Party. By 1921 he was strong enough to challenge Drexler and take over the leadership of the Party himself.

Source E: A photograph of Nazi supporters in Bavaria, 1920. Hitler is second from the left.

Source F: Karl Luedecke, one of Hitler's earliest supporters, describing an early meeting of the newly formed Nazi Party.

> 'When he spoke of Germany's disgrace, I felt ready to spring at an enemy. His appeal to the honour of German manhood was like a call to arms, and the gospel he preached a sacred revelation… I forgot everything but this man. When I looked around, I saw that his power of suggestion was magnetising those as one. I had an experience which was comparable to a religious conviction.'

Activities

8 What can you learn from Source F about Hitler's qualities as a speaker?

9 Explain how Hitler had managed to become leader of the Nazi Party by 1921.

What were the main features of the early Nazi Party, 1920–1922?

The Nazi Party was based in Munich but it soon began to spread to other parts of Germany. The Nazis published their own newspapers to spread their ideas and received support from extreme nationalists and anti-communists. By 1922 the Nazi Party had 6,000 members, rising to 50,000 two years later.

The swastika

Hitler himself designed the Nazi flag with the *swastika* symbol. The three colours, red, white and black, had been the colours of the German flag under the *Kaiser*. Red represented the socialist part of the Party, the white the nationalist and the *swastika* itself Hitler's racial views.

Hitler

Hitler's personal qualities, especially as an **orator**, encouraged many to join the Nazi Party. He put great faith in the spoken word, and stage-managed and rehearsed his speeches carefully. He would use a long and gradual build-up to increase the anticipation of the audience. He practised his gestures and studied photographs of himself in action. The SA, Hitler's personal bodyguard, were there to deal with hecklers.

Source G: A supporter describes a Nazi meeting in 1926.

'A storm of jubilation rising from afar, from the street and moving into the lobby, announced the coming of the *Führer*. And then suddenly the auditorium went wild, as he strode resolutely in his raincoat and without a hat to the rostrum. When the speech came to an end I could not see out of my eyes any more. There were tears in my eyes, my throat was all tight from crying… I looked round discreetly, and noticed that others, too, men and women and young fellows were as deeply affected as I.'

Source H: A painting of Hitler speaking to a Nazi Party meeting in 1921.

The SA

In 1921 Hitler set up the *Sturm Abteilung* (SA) (also known as the stormtroopers). It attracted many ex-soldiers, especially from the *Freikorps*. These were men who felt betrayed by the Treaty of Versailles. The SA would disrupt the meetings of Hitler's opponents, especially the communists, and often beat up opposition supporters. They were also known as the 'Brownshirts' because of the colour of their uniform. Ernst Röhm, one of the founder members of the German Workers' Party in 1919, became the leader of the SA.

The Party programme

The Nazi Party programme was kept vague and deliberately designed to appeal to as many groups as possible:

- Nationalism appealed with the promise to destroy the Treaty of Versailles and introduce rearmament.
- Socialism appealed to the workers. The Nazis promised to give workers a share in company profits, to nationalise big companies, and to share out land for the benefit of everyone.
- Anti-Semitism or hatred of the Jews appealed to those Germans who needed a scapegoat for Germany's defeat in the First World War and also those who were resentful of Jewish wealth.
- Hitler hated communism and promised to remove the threat from the German Communist Party. This

appealed to the middle classes and big business: both of these groups would lose out if the communists took over the German government.

examzone

Build better answers

Why did the Nazi Party gain support in the years 1919-1922? Explain your answer. You may use the following in your answer:

• the influence of Hitler
• the Nazi Party programme

You must also include information of your own. (16 marks)

■ Basic, Level 1

Answer makes generalised statements without support from detail OR gives detail on a limited aspect of the question.

● Good, Level 2

Answer gives a narrative of what happened that is mostly relevant and accurate, without referring to the focus of the question, for example: the fact that Hitler had a powerful personality, or that the Nazi Party programme targeted different groups, without explaining how this might lead to increased membership. Better answers also refer to information outside the bullet points.

● Better, Level 3

Answer understands the focus of the question and uses detail about the bullet points to support their answer, for example: *Hitler was a powerful speaker and could convince people to join the Nazi Party.* Better answers also include information that is not in the question: for example, reasons why people wanted to join the SA.

▲ Excellent, Level 4

Answer uses accurate detail from the bullet points and own knowledge to analyse the question and evaluate the impact of the various reasons they consider, for example explaining the attraction of points on the Nazi Party programme such as anti-Semitism or nationalism. To reach this level, students must use information of their own.

Make sure you write accurately – there are four extra marks available for spelling, grammar and punctuation in these questions.

Activities

10 Read Source G and remind yourself of your answer to Question 8.

  a) Does Source G support the answer you gave to Question 8? Explain your answer.

  b) Does this mean that Hitler's speeches had the same effect on everyone who went to hear them?

11 a) How might the activities of the SA lead to the Nazis gaining support?

  b) How might the SA lose the Nazis' support?

12 'The Weimar Republic was doomed to failure from the very start.' Discuss.

Summary

• The Weimar Republic was set up after the revolution of November 1918. It introduced a new constitution, which had several weaknesses, especially the use of proportional representation, which encouraged weak coalition governments.

• The new republic got off to a bad start because it had to sign the Treaty of Versailles. This Treaty was unpopular with many Germans because of its harsh terms, especially the War Guilt clause and the payment of reparations.

• The Weimar Republic survived two attempts to overthrow it, one from the left and one from the right: the Spartacist uprising of January 1919 and the Kapp *Putsch* of March 1920.

• In 1921 Hitler became leader of the Nazi Party, which by 1921 had its own private army, the SA, and was preparing for an armed uprising.

1918

Abdication of Kaiser William II

Armistice

1919

Hitler joins German Workers' Party

Spartacist uprising

Treaty of Versailles

1920

Kapp *Putsch*

German Workers' Party renamed Nazi Party

1921

Hitler becomes leader of the Nazi Party

1.2 Challenges and recovery 1923-1929

Learning outcomes

By the end of this topic you should be able to:

- understand the causes and effects of the hyperinflation of 1923
- explain the importance of the Munich *Putsch* of 1923
- describe how far the Weimar Republic recovered in the years 1924–1929.

Hyperinflation: When prices go up very quickly

Passive resistance: To resist authority in a peaceful, non-violent way

The Ruhr: The industrial part of Germany producing coal, iron and steel

Source A: Women and children on a coal tip in Germany in 1923.

Getting an overview

French troops seize the Ruhr

In January 1923 French troops occupied the Ruhr industrial area of Germany because the German government was unable to make its first reparations payment. The Weimar Republic was power-less to do anything although German workers in the Ruhr used passive resistance by refusing to work for the French and factories came to a standstill.

Revolution in a Beer Hall

In November 1923 Hitler and the SA raided a Beer Hall in Munich and captured two of the leaders of Bavaria. They hoped to persuade them to support a Nazi takeover. The leaders escaped and the revolution was defeated. Hitler was arrested and put on trial. He was sentenced to five years in prison but only served nine months during which he wrote his autobiography, *Mein Kampf.*

The *mark* is worthless

By November 1923 Germany was suffering from hyper-inflation. The German *mark* became worthless and it cost one and half million *marks* for a loaf of bread. Many people lost all of their savings whilst workers and pensioners were unable to buy everyday necessities. The Weimar Republic became more unpopular than ever.

Germany recovers under Stresemann

Germany recovered from the disasters of 1923 mainly due to the leadership of the Foreign Secretary, Gustav Stresemann. He reduced inflation by introducing the *Rentenmark*. He also reduced reparation payments through the Dawes and Young Plans and encouraged the USA to make loans to German industry. Germany was allowed to join the League of Nations and, once again, became an important power.

Activities

1 Study Source A. What are the women and children doing in this photograph?

2 What impression does the photograph give about Germany in 1923?

3 Match the following alternative headlines to the newspaper cuttings shown in the overview above:

- The USA rescues Germany
- Prices rocket out of control
- Workers refuse to co-operate with invaders
- Munich fiasco.

The invasion of the Ruhr

Why did French troops invade the Ruhr in 1923?

The German government had been unable to make its first reparations payment in 1922. Instead, it requested extra time for the payment, but France refused. Therefore, in January 1923, the French marched into **the Ruhr** industrial area of Germany, determined to get payment in kind for the money owed.

Source B: A French magazine cover showing French soldiers in the Ruhr in January 1923. The caption at the foot reads: 'At the gates of every public building and factory, the blue helmets of our soldiers remind the forgetful Germans of France's rightful claims.'

How did Germany react to the occupation?

The German government was unable to offer any armed resistance. Instead, the workers chose **passive resistance** and went on strike, refusing to work for the foreign army of occupation. Some even took more direct action. They set some of the factories on fire and sabotaged the pumps in some mines so they flooded and could not be worked. There were clashes with the French troops and a number of strikers were shot.

Source C: An official French army account of the occupation.

'Passive resistance meant not co-operating at all with the French and Belgians. It meant refusing all their demands and orders. The post, the telegraph and telephone workers would have nothing to do with the French and Belgians, to send their letters, to sell them stamps, and so on. Railway workers refused to run the trains needed for the troops.'

What were the effects of the invasion?

The invasion had mixed effects. It united the German people against the French invaders, with the strikers being seen as heroes of the German people. The popularity of the Weimar temporarily increased because it had backed the strikers and organised passive resistance. Nevertheless, it had disastrous effects on the German economy. The government had to print more money to pay the strikers, which in turn increased inflation. The strike meant fewer goods were produced and this made inflation even worse.

Activities

1 Study Source B. Imagine this was to be published in a German magazine. Devise an alternative caption.

2 Do you agree that the French were justified in occupying the Ruhr?

3 'A political success but an economic disaster.'
   How far do you agree with this view of the effects of the French occupation of the Ruhr on Germany?

Why did Germany suffer from hyperinflation in 1923?

Hyperinflation is when a government prints too much paper money. Because there is so much money in circulation, it loses its value rapidly. This causes prices to shoot up. As things become more expensive, for the people and the government, the government can feel pushed to print even more money – even though printing money caused the problem in the first place. A number of things pushed the Weimar government to keep printing money:

- During the First World War they needed money to pay for the war.
- After the First World War they needed money to pay reparations.
- With the French invasion of the Ruhr, more money still was needed.

Source A: The value of the *mark* against the US dollar, 1919-1923.

Year	Number of *marks* to a dollar
1919	9
January 1921	65
July 1922	493
January 1923	17,972
November 1923	4.2 billion

Activities

1 What is meant by hyperinflation?
2 Working in pairs, organise the effects of hyperinflation into:
   - those who gained
   - those who lost.
3 Do you agree that the French occupation of the Ruhr was the most important cause of hyperinflation? Explain your reasons.

The occupation of the Ruhr

The Ruhr, Germany's main industrial area, produced 80% of Germany's iron and coal output and contained many factories. When the French occupied it in January 1923, they took raw materials, goods and machinery as part-payment of reparations and seemed determined to stay until they were fully paid. Workers offered passive resistance - they worked slowly or went on strike. Some sabotaged factories or transport routes. This increased Germany's debts whilst reducing income, and created further unemployment and shortages of goods. The government printed more money. In 1923, the German government had 300 paper mills and 2,000 printing shops doing nothing but print money.

Source B: Children stacking up German banknotes. Hyperinflation had made real banknotes almost worthless.

Massive price rises

Wages could not keep up with price rises.

This table shows what happened to the price of bread in Berlin (prices in *marks*):

July 1923	3,465
August 1923	69,000
September 1923	1,512,000
October 1923	1,743,000,000
November 1923	201,000,000,000

Businessmen

Many businessmen who had borrowed money from the banks were able to wipe out their debts. Others were able to take over smaller businesses that were going bankrupt.

Fixed incomes

People on fixed incomes, such as pensions, found that they became worthless.

Farmers

Farmers benefited from the rise in prices of food at a time when the farming industry was not doing well.

Effects of hyperinflation

Workers

Those in employment were generally secure because wages went higher and higher. However, wage rises always lagged behind price rises.

German money became worthless

Some people had been saving for years. These savings became worthless.

The rich

They usually had land and possessions and were protected from the worst effects of hyperinflation.

The middle class

Many lost faith in the Weimar Republic and were convinced that it was unable to deal with serious economic problems.

What were the effects of hyperinflation?

Hyperinflation hit people who relied on their savings, because they became worthless. Pensioners who were on a fixed pension found that it bought them less and less. People who relied on wages also suffered, as wages rose slower than prices. In late 1923, the price of food or fuel went up so fast that some employers paid their workers twice a day, so they could shop earlier in the day, before prices rose again.

Hyperinflation benefitted some people. Some farmers made enough from the rise in food prices to more than cope with other prices rising. People who had loans and mortgages were sometimes able to pay them off and rent became cheaper. Some businesses were able to pay off loans and buy up smaller, failing, businesses cheaply.

Activities

4   In groups of three, prepare a role-play about the effects of hyperinflation on three different people (a farmer, a pensioner, a housewife, a worker etc.) in Germany in November 1923. Think what their attitude to the Weimer government would be.

5   In pairs, draw a balance sheet of the effects of hyperinflation on German people.

6   In groups, prepare arguments for and against the three options facing the Weimar government during and after the First World War – raise taxes, borrow money or print money.

7   To what extent was printing money the least of the three evils?

8   'The hyperinflation of 1923 was a disaster for all Germans.' Discuss.

Why did Hitler carry out the Munich Putsch?

In 1923, Hitler and the Nazis tried to take over in Germany. They did this by starting a 'putsch', a military takeover, in Munich. Why a putsch in 1923? Why start it in Munich?

Source A: A Bavarian police report, written in September 1923.

'As a result of rising prices and increasing unemployment, the workers are bitter. The patriotic bands are at fever pitch because of the abandonment of the Ruhr resistance.'

Hitler's aims

He was determined to overthrow the Weimar Republic by organising a successful revolution in Bavaria and then, with his supporters, organising a march on Berlin.

Influence of Mussolini

The Italian leader, Benito Mussolini, had successfully marched on Rome the previous year and taken over the Italian government.

Bavarian leaders

The Bavarian government was right wing. Its leaders, Gustav von Kahr and General von Lossow, had been plotting against the Weimar Republic. Hitler was convinced that they would support a putsch.

Discontent in Germany

The timing seemed ideal for an armed uprising. The Weimar Republic was more unpopular than ever due to the terrible effects of hyperinflation. Moreover, many nationalists were incensed when, in September 1923, Stresemann's government called off passive resistance in the Ruhr and resumed paying reparations to the French.

Reasons for the Munich Putsch

The Nazi Party

The Nazi Party appeared ready to seize power by force. Hitler was the established leader, it had 50,000 supporters and its own private army, the SA. In addition, Hitler had developed an increasingly close relationship with the former army leader, General Ludendorff. Hitler believed that Ludendorff would be able to persuade the German army to desert the government and side with the Nazis.

Source B: A report by the Munich city council in October 1923.

'In all of Munich (including the food market) absolutely no potatoes have been available for days which, in view of the fact that potatoes are naturally the cheapest food, is particularly tragic at this time.'

Activities

1 Why would the reports written in Sources A and B have encouraged Hitler to carry out the uprising?
2 How did the following people encourage Hitler to carry out the uprising?
   a) Mussolini
   b) Ludendorff
   c) Gustav von Kahr.

Events of the Putsch

The Munich Putsch began on 8 November. Hitler and the SA burst into a beer hall where the head of the Bavarian government, Gustav von Kahr, was holding a meeting. Hitler jumped onto a table, announced he was taking over the government of Bavaria and tried to persuade everyone there to join him. They were unwilling, despite threats, until von Ludendorff arrived and said he supported the Putsch. They then agreed to support the Putsch and were released.

Source C: An eyewitness description.

'Hitler climbed onto a chair to my left. The hall was still restless. Hitler made a sign to the man on his right, who fired a shot at the ceiling. Thereupon Hitler called out: "The national revolution has broken out. The hall is surrounded." He asked Kahr and the other two gentlemen to come out of the room nearby. He guaranteed their personal freedom… Throughout this time, Hitler was radiant with joy. One had the feeling that he was delighted to have succeeded in persuading Kahr to work with him. I would say he had a childlike joy, which I will never forget. By comparison, Ludendorff looked extremely grave and pale. He had the appearance of a man who knew it was a matter of life or death.'

9 November 1923

Hitler and Ludendorff, with about 3,000 supporters (many of whom were SA members), marched through Munich, hoping to win mass public support. They were also expecting von Kahr and many other people from the beer hall meeting to join them as they marched. Instead, as they neared the city centre, they were met by armed police, who tried to turn them back.

There are several versions of what happened next. Certainly a shot was fired, but no one knows who fired this shot. The first shot was followed by a gun battle between the marchers and the police. It only lasted about a minute, during which 16 marchers and three policemen were killed. During the gun battle, Hitler fell to the ground. He may have been pushed or tripped. He may have dived to the ground to avoid the bullets. Hitler then fled, as did many of the SA. Ludendorff gave himself up.

The aftermath

Hitler was arrested on 11 November. He was put on trial for his part in the uprising, along with Ludendorff and eight others. They were accused of high treason. Hitler turned the trial into a propaganda success. He admitted to starting the *Putsch*, but said it was not high treason because it could not be treason to act against the government that had signed the Treaty of Versailles.

Newspapers all over Germany, and world-wide, reported his speech, especially his assertion that his uprising was to overthrow the Weimar Republic for their betrayal of the German people. The court was sympathetic to him and the other conspirators. The maximum sentence for high treason was execution. The minimum sentence was five years in prison. Ludendorff was acquitted. The court gave Hitler the minimum sentence. The other eight were also given short prison sentences. However, the Nazi Party was banned as a result of the *Putsch*.

Source D: A painting made later by one of Hitler's followers who took part in the Munich *Putsch*. In the foreground the police are opening fire on the Nazis. Hitler stands with his arm raised with Ludendorff on his right.

Activities

3 Does the painting shown in Source D give an accurate view of the events of the Munich uprising? Explain your answer.

4 Suggest two reasons for the failure of the uprising.

Imprisonment

Hitler was imprisoned in Landsberg Prison, but had a room of his own and as many visitors as he wanted. He spent much of his time writing *Mein Kampf* (My Struggle) – an autobiography and a list of aims and policies for the Nazi Party. The main points for the Party were:

- the removal of all Jews from Germany
- the destruction of communism
- Germany's expansion east to create more 'living space' (**lebensraum**) for Germany.

After just nine months, Hitler was freed.

Source E: From Hitler's evidence at his trial (following the Munich *Putsch*), February 1924.

> 'I alone bear responsibility for the *putsch* but I am not a criminal because of that. There is no such thing as high treason among the traitors of 1918. I only wanted what's best for the German people. I only wanted to lead Germany back to honour, to its proper position in the world. I only wish I had suffered the same fate as my dear slaughtered colleagues.'

Activities

5 Why was Hitler given such a short prison sentence?

6 Copy and complete the ideas map below. Highlight the consequence you think was the most important and explain your choice.

Consequences of the Munich *Putsch*

7 Study Source G. Do you agree with the views expressed by Hitler? Explain your answer.

8 Draw up a table summarising the challenges faced by the Weimar government up to 1924. Include a comment on how and why it was able to survive each challenge.

Was the uprising a failure?

The uprising appeared to have been a disastrous and humiliating failure. Hitler had failed to win the support of Kahr, the Bavarian army and the police. He had run away from the gun battle of 9 November, but then been arrested. He was found guilty at his trial and spent nine months in prison.

However, there were some positive consequences for Hitler and the Nazi Party, more especially from his trial.

Hitler also made use of his trial to attack the Weimar Republic and ensure maximum publicity for himself throughout Germany. In addition, the failure prompted Hitler to rethink his tactics, realising that a future armed uprising would be doomed to failure.

Source F: Hitler speaking in the mid 1920s.

> 'Instead of working to achieve power by an armed coup, we shall have to hold our noses and enter the *Reichstag* against the opposition deputies. If outvoting them takes longer than outshooting them, at least the results will be guaranteed by their own constitution. Sooner or later we shall have a majority and after that – Germany.'

Hitler himself believed that the failure was a blessing in disguise.

Source G: From a speech by Hitler in 1933.

> 'It was the greatest good fortune for us Nazis that the *putsch* collapsed because:
>
> 1 The sudden takeover of power in the whole of Germany would have led to the greatest difficulties in 1923 because the essential preparations had not even been begun by the Nationalist Socialist Party.
>
> 2 Most important of all, the bloody sacrifice of 9 November 1923 has proven the most effective propaganda for National Socialism.'

The recovery of the Republic, 1924–1929

During the years 1924 to 1929 the Weimar Republic appeared to recover from the disasters of 1923.

The period even became known as '**the Golden Years**', when Germany gained confidence and international acceptance.

Reasons for recovery	Evidence of recovery
The recovery was due to several factors: • Gustav Stresemann, who was Foreign Secretary, played a leading role, especially in sorting out reparations and hyperinflation • The Dawes Plan of 1924 reduced Germany's reparations • US loans to Germany • The Young Plan of 1929 further reduced reparations payments, which were to be paid over a period of 58 years • Stresemann introduced a new currency called the *rentenmark*, which ended hyperinflation • In 1925 Germany signed the Locarno Treaties, which outlawed the use of force to alter the Belgium-German and Franco-German borders. Britain and Italy guaranteed the agreement • In 1926 Germany was allowed to join the League of Nations.	• There was little support for extremist parties such as the Nazis, who only won twelve seats in the elections of 1928 • There was more support for parties such as the Social Democrats, who supported the Republic • Germany was accepted again as an important power in Europe • New factories were built • There was a fall in unemployment • New roads and railways were built, as well as nearly 3 million new homes • Prosperity was shown by new airships, ocean liners, radio stations and film studios • Foreign banks, especially in the US, lent nearly 25,000 billion *marks* to German borrowers.

Source A: 1920s Berlin.

Activities

1 Look at Source A. Make a list of evidence of prosperity in Germany in the 1920s.

2 Draw two spider diagrams:
   a) one showing reasons for recovery
   b) the other giving examples of recovery.

3 Use your diagrams and Source A to write a paragraph explaining why 'the Golden Years' might be an accurate description of the Weimar Republic during 1924-29.

What was the role of Stresemann?

There has been much debate about why Germany recovered in the years 1924–1929, especially concerning the importance of the part played by Gustav Stresemann. He was a very good speaker and administrator and, in August 1923, was appointed Chancellor in order to deal with the problems of hyperinflation. It was his decision to call off passive resistance in the Ruhr. However, by November 1923, he had lost the support of the *Reichstag* as Chancellor. Instead, he became Foreign Secretary until his death in October 1929.

Stresemann followed a policy of fulfilment: this meant co-operating with France and Britain in order to remove or reduce some of the terms of the Treaty of Versailles, especially reparations. He outlined his aims in a letter to the son of the former Kaiser William II, in September 1925.

Source B: From Stresemann's letter to the former *Kaiser's* son.

> 'In my opinion there are three great tasks that confront German foreign policy in the immediate future:
>
> 1 The solution of the reparations problem in a way that is tolerable for Germany.
>
> 2 The protection of those ten to twelve million Germans who now live under foreign control in foreign lands.
>
> 3 The readjustment of our eastern frontiers; the recovery of Danzig, the Polish Corridor, and a correction of the frontier in Upper Silesia.'

Stabilising the *mark*

He was responsible for a number of measures to deal with Germany's problems. The hyperinflation of 1923 had destroyed the value of the German mark. In order to stabilise the currency, Stresemann introduced a temporary currency called the *rentenmark* in November 1923. This was issued in limited numbers, and had its value based not on gold reserves but on a mortgage of Germany's entire industrial and agricultural resources. In other words, a *rentenmark* could, in theory, be exchanged for a piece of land or industry. This did not happen, because the German people showed confidence in the new currency. In the following year, the *rentenmark* was converted into the *reichsmark*, another new currency, now backed with gold.

This measure gradually restored the value of the *mark*, stabilised the German financial system and greatly reduced inflation.

Improving foreign relations

Stresemann greatly improved relations with Britain and France by ending passive resistance in the Ruhr and signing the Locarno Treaties of 1925. These Treaties prohibited the use of violence when dealing with the Belgium-German and Franco-German borders. The period 1925–1929 became known as the 'Locarno Honeymoon' and furthered Stresemann's policy of fulfilment, co-operation abroad to reduce reparations and further German economic recovery. Indeed, in 1926 Stresemann was awarded the Nobel Peace Prize.

Source C: A poster urging voters to reject the Young Plan. It says: 'You must slave into the third generation.'

Also in 1926, Stresemann took Germany into the League of Nations. Germany was recognised as a great power and given a permanent seat on the League's council alongside France and Britain.

In 1928, Germany signed the Kellogg-Briand Pact along with 64 other nations. It was agreed that they would keep their armies for self-defence but would solve all future disputes by 'peaceful means'. Peace would further assist German economic recovery and growth.

What other reasons were there for recovery?

There were other reasons for German economic recovery, especially the Dawes and Young Plans and loans from the United States.

The Dawes Plan

The Dawes Plan of 1924, negotiated between the USA and Germany, but with the support of France and Britain, reorganised Germany's reparation payments. These were not only reduced but were also more sensibly staged to match Germany's capacity to pay. For the first five years, German payments would start at £50 million, increasing to £150 million over the five-year period. Thereafter, the payments would be linked to Germany's capacity to pay. In return, the French withdrew their troops from the Ruhr.

Furthermore, the Dawes Plan included a US loan of 800 million gold *marks* to Germany. Over the following six years, Germany borrowed about $3,000 million from US banks. This greatly assisted the growth of German industry as well as the payment of reparations. German nationalists opposed the Dawes Plan, which they described as 'a second Versailles'. They resented the Dawes Plan because it gave the Allies partial control over Germany's railways and the German state bank.

Moreover, it was an admission that Germany had caused the war, which they totally disagreed with.

The Young Plan

In 1929, Germany negotiated a further change to reparations, known as the Young Plan. For the first time a timescale for reparations repayments was set, with Germany making repayments for the next 59 years until 1988. The repayments were fixed at 2,000 million *marks* a year (reduced from the 2,500 million *marks* set by the Dawes Plan). In addition, responsibility for repayment was given to Germany, rather than the Allies. In return for this agreement, the French promised to evacuate the Rhineland by June 1930, five years ahead of schedule.

However, there was strong opposition to the Young Plan from nationalist groups, who were against any further payments of reparations, especially staged over so many years. Alfred Hugenberg, a media tycoon, supported by Hitler and the Nazis, formed the Reich Committee for a Referendum to oppose the Young Plan and raised a petition with 4 million signatures. A referendum was held in December 1929 and resulted in defeat for those who opposed the Young Plan with only 5.8 million or 14 per cent voting to reject it.

Activities

4 In pairs, study Source C.
   a) What is the message of the poster?
   b) What arguments would the supporters of the Young Plan make in reply to this poster?

5 Explain the importance of Stresemann's role in the recovery of the Republic in the years 1923 to 1929.

Think about ending the crisis in the Ruhr, stabilising the currency, improving foreign relationships, and the Dawes and Young Plans.

6 What was the most important reason for German recovery, 1924–1929?

Make a copy of the following table. Complete the table indicating the level of importance of each person or agreement, giving a brief explanation in the right-hand column.

	Quite important	Important	Very important	Decisive	Reason
Stresemann					
Dawes Plan					
Young Plan					
US loans					

To what extent did the Weimar Republic recover?

Although Germany appeared to recover in the years 1924–1929, there has been much debate about the extent of this recovery. Even people at the time could not agree, as can be seen in Sources D and E.

Source D: A German journalist writing in 1929.

'In comparison with what we expected after Versailles, Germany has raised herself up to shoulder the terrific burden of peace in a way we should never have thought possible. The spirit of Versailles has been conquered.'

Source E: Stresemann, speaking in 1929.

'The economic position is only flourishing on the surface. Germany is in fact dancing on a volcano. If the short term loans are called in by the USA, a large section of our economy would collapse.'

Activities

7 'As a result of the work of Stresemann between 1924 and 1929, the Weimar Republic fully recovered from the problems it had faced in its first four years.' Discuss.

Political recovery

For recovery	Against recovery
1 The period saw more stable government After the 1928 election, the Social Democrats joined a coalition government for the first time since 1923	1 The basic problems of the constitution remained No one party could secure a majority in the *Reichstag* and there were frequent, short-lived coalition governments
2 Stresemann was a popular leader with many Germans	2 Many nationalists opposed the Dawes and Young Plans
3 There was little support for extremist parties For example, the Nazis only won twelve seats in the 1928 election	3 Extremist parties such as the Nazis and communists were determined to overthrow the Weimar Republic
4 Hindenburg, who was a popular First World War leader, was elected President in 1925 He promised to maintain the constitution.	4 Hindenburg, who was elected President in 1925, disliked the new republic.

Economic recovery

For recovery	Against recovery
1 The new *rentenmark* stabilised the German currency	1 German recovery was too dependent on US loans This was to prove disastrous after the **Wall Street Crash**
2 US loans encouraged the growth of German industry By 1928 industrial production finally reached pre-war levels By 1930 Germany was one of the leading exporters of manufactured goods	2 Unemployment remained a serious problem The economy was not growing fast enough for Germany's rising population
3 Industrial recovery brought more employment	3 Growth in industry began to slow down after 1927
4 In nearly every town new factories and public facilities sprang up New roads and railways were built as well as nearly 3 million new homes.	4 Farming suffered from depression throughout the 1920s because of a fall in food prices Furthermore, income from agriculture went down in the period 1925–1929.

Activities

8 'The years 1924–1929 saw political stability and economic recovery in Germany.' From the evidence of this section how far do you agree/disagree with this view? Complete the scales below for both political and economic recovery.

   a) Identify the evidence that supports this view

   b) Identify the evidence that does not support this view.

   Decide how much you agree – and explain why.

9 How important was the role of Stresemann in the recovery of the Republic in the years 1924–1929? Make a copy of and complete the following table.

Use this to make your judgement on the importance of the role of Stresemann in Germany's recovery, giving your reasons.

Achievements	Limitations

Evidence for   Evidence against

Summary

- In 1923 the Weimar Republic suffered its worst year. The French occupied the Ruhr in order to force reparations payments from Germany. This worsened Germany's economic problems and triggered hyperinflation.

- Hitler joined and later led the Nazi Party in order to overthrow the Weimar Republic. By 1923, it had its own private army known as the SA and was ready to seize power.

- The Munich *Putsch* of 1923 was a failure. Hitler was arrested and put in prison. However, he gained much publicity from his trial.

- The Weimar Republic seemed to recover in the years 1924 to 1929 mainly as a result of the work of Stresemann.

31

1923
French occupation of the Ruhr

Hyperinflation

Munich *Putsch*

1924
Dawes Plan

Introduction of *rentenmark*

1925
Locarno Treaties

1926
Germany joins the League of Nations

1928
Kellogg-Briand Pact

1929
Young Plan

Death of Stresemann

1.3 Support for the Nazi Party 1923-1932

Learning outcomes

By the end of this topic you should be able to:

 understand which groups supported the Nazi Party in the years 1921–1928

● explain why there was greater support for the Nazis in the years 1929–1932

● describe which groups supported the Nazis in the years 1929–1932.

Propaganda: False or misleading information given out to spread certain points of view

Wall Street Crash: Wall Street is the home of the New York stock exchange. Share prices fell disastrously on Wall Street in October 1929

Getting an overview

1924

32 seats

The Nazi Party did quite well in the first election they contested for the *Reichstag*. This was at least partly because of the publicity provided by Hitler's trial. Many Germans were still unhappy about the events of 1923, especially hyperinflation. Hitler began to reorganise the Nazi Party ready to fight future general elections. The main support came from middle-class people who were frightened of communism.

1928

12 seats

The election results of 1928 proved disappointing for the Nazis, but were not surprising. This was the period of recovery under Stresemann, with few voters prepared to support extreme parties such as the Nazis or communists.

1930

107 seats

Within two years the Nazis had become the second largest party in the *Reichstag*. This was due to the disastrous effects of the Wall Street Crash on Germany. It led to a terrible depression in German industry, with unemployment reaching 4 million by 1930. Many of Hitler's supporters were from the middle classes, who feared a communist takeover.

1932

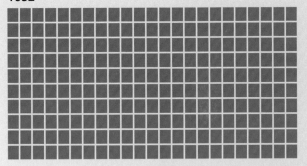

230 seats

In July 1932 the Nazis became the largest party in the *Reichstag*. Increased support was again due to the effects of the depression, with unemployment peaking at 6 million. The Nazis skilfully exploited the depression by using both clever propaganda (organised by Josef Goebbels) and the personal appeal of Hitler himself to win over as many groups as possible. The organisation and discipline of the SA impressed many Germans. The Nazis also attracted support from big businesses, the middle classes and some of the unemployed.

Source A: People cutting up the carcass of a horse in a street in Berlin in 1931.

Activities

1 Draw a bar chart to show the seats won by the Nazis in 1924, 1928, 1930 and 1932.

2 For each year, give one reason for the Nazi result.

3 What does Source A suggest about the lifestyle of German people in 1931?

Build better answers

What can you learn from Source A about the effects of the depression in Germany? **(4 marks)**

■ **Basic, Level 1**
Answer makes an inference but does not use the source to support it, for example: *people were hungry, or people were out of work.*

● **Good, Level 2**
Answer uses the source to support the inference, for example: *the source suggests that they were desperate for food, otherwise they would not be cutting the horse up. If people were so very hungry, it suggests they were out of work and had no money for food.*

How was the Nazi Party reorganised in the years 1924–1928?

The Nazi Party had been banned after the Munich *Putsch*, but in February 1925 the ban was lifted and Hitler relaunched the Party. It was totally reorganised into a party that could appeal to the electors and win seats in the *Reichstag*. He also turned it into a national party that was active throughout Germany, not just Bavaria.

Bamberg Conference

Hitler survived threats to his leadership of the Party from Gregor Strasser and Josef Goebbels. They wanted the Party to become more socialist in order to appeal to the working classes. Hitler was opposed to this and called a Party conference in Bamberg in Bavaria in 1926. His leadership was confirmed and Goebbels became one of his closest supporters.

Nazi organisations

These were set up to appeal to certain interest groups, including the Nazi Students' League, the Teachers' League and the Women's League. The Nazi youth movement was organised to appeal to the young.

Party rallies

In 1926 a Nazi Party rally was held at Weimar. This began the pattern of military-style parades.

Party organisation

Hitler reorganised the Party to make it more efficient and to ensure it was prepared, even at street level, to fight future elections. He created a national headquarters in Munich and insisted on the central control of finance and membership. Branches of the Party, known as *Gaus*, were set up all over Germany and were placed under the control of a Party official known as a *Gauleiter*.

The SA

This was strengthened with more young men encouraged to join. The image of the organisation was changed, placing the emphasis on discipline and order rather than violence and intimidation.

Agricultural areas

From 1928, the Nazis focused much more on winning support in agricultural areas. This was because of the depression, which had affected farming throughout the 1920s and worsened in 1927 with a further slump in food prices.

Mein Kampf

Hitler's book, *Mein Kampf*, was published in 1925 and, because of the publicity from Hitler's trial, it became a best seller.

Propaganda

Goebbels organised Party **propaganda** and used posters skilfully. He also used Nazi newspapers and meetings to put across the Nazi ideals. He discovered that their anti-Jewish message had most appeal among the working classes and increased anti-Semitic propaganda. The Nazis were the only party to run evening classes to train their members in public-speaking skills.

Source A: A Nazi election poster of 1924. The poster shows a figure representing Germany with a Jewish banker on his shoulders.

Who were the Nazi Party's early supporters?

The Nazi Party appears to have attracted support from the following main groups:

- A high proportion of younger members who were either ex-soldiers or were too young to have fought in the First World War greatly admired Hitler. Some of these were university students.
- Middle-class groups such as master craftsmen, clerks and merchants, who lost out in 1923 due to hyperinflation and felt threatened by communism.
- Farmers who were badly affected by the fall in food prices of the 1920s and the onset of a depression in agriculture from 1927.
- Skilled workers such as plumbers and electricians.

Although membership of the Party increased to over 100,000 by 1928, the Nazis did not do well in the *Reichstag* elections. Having won 32 seats in May 1924, four years later this fell to 12 seats. This was due to the revival of the Republic under Stresemann.

Source B: William Shirer, an American journalist living in Germany, gave this verdict on the Nazis after the elections of 1928.

'Nazism appears to be a dying cause. It got support because of the country's problems such as hyperinflation and the French invasion of the Ruhr. Now that the country's outlook is bright it is dying away. One scarcely hears of Hitler except as the butt of jokes.'

Activities

3 Study Source B. Do you agree with Shirer's views about the Nazi Party in 1928? Explain your answer.

4 Make a copy of the following table and then complete it with some reasons that these three groups of people may have for supporting the Nazis.

Group	Possible reasons to support Nazis
Young people	
Farmers	
Merchants	

What effects did the depression have on Germany?

From October 1929, Germany was badly affected by an economic depression. This further weakened the Weimar Republic and provided Hitler and the Nazis with the ideal opportunity to increase their support.

SHARES ON WALL STREET CRASH

Wall Street Crash
In October 1929 disaster struck the New York stock exchange on Wall Street. The value of the shares collapsed following a few days of wild speculation. Many US businesses were ruined and the Americans had no option but to end their loans to Germany and demand the repayment of existing loans.

German businessmen
Many German businesses were forced to close. They were heavily dependent on loans from the USA. To make matters worse, the government increased their taxes in order to pay for helping the rapidly increasing numbers of unemployed.

German workers
Many workers and farm labourers lost their jobs. By 1932, six million were out of work, including 40% of factory workers. At the same time the government cut unemployment benefit to save money. Many families suffered terrible poverty.

Weimar Republic
Most Germans blamed the Weimar Republic for allowing the German economy to become far too dependent on US loans. In addition, the government was criticised for its failure to deal with the worst effects of the depression, especially high unemployment.

German young people
Unemployment badly affected the young. By the end of 1932, half of Germans between sixteen and thirty could not find jobs, including 60% of university graduates.

Source A: A graph showing unemployment in Germany, 1928–1936.

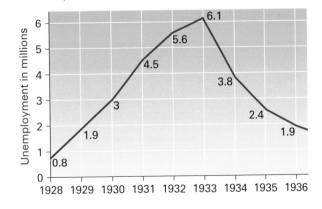

Activities

1. What was the **Wall Street Crash**?
2. Study Source A. When did unemployment reach its peak?
3. Make a list of at least three effects of the depression on Germany.
4. 'The Weimar Republic was unable to manage economic problems in Germany in the years 1919–1932.' Discuss.

36

Source B: The writer Heinrich Hauser describes what he saw as he toured Germany in 1932.

'An almost unbroken chain of homeless men extends the whole length of the Hamburg–Berlin highway. It is the same scene for the entire two hundred miles, and all the highways in Germany over which I travelled this year. They walked separately or in small groups with their eyes on the ground. And they had the strange, stumbling gait of barefoot people, for their shoes were slung over their shoulders.'

Activities

5 What can you learn from Source B about the effects of the depression on Germany?

6 Who suffered the most during the depression? Explain your answer.

Why was the Weimar Republic weakened by the depression?

The Weimar Republic was weakened for several reasons.

- It lacked a strong leader to reduce the worst effects of the depression. Stresemann, who might have provided such strong leadership, died just a few weeks before the Wall Street Crash.
- The Weimar constitution had encouraged weak and short-lived coalitions, unable to provide solutions to major problems, and the depression highlighted these weaknesses.

Activities

7 'The Wall Street Crash was to blame for the economic and social problems of Germany in the years 1929–1932.'

From the evidence, how far do you agree or disagree with this opinion? Work in groups and consider the following:

- the impact of the Wall Street Crash
- German policies 1924–1929
- the actions of the Weimar governments 1929–1932.

examzone **Watch out!**

Many students get confused between the Wall Street Crash of 1929 and hyperinflation in 1923. Make sure that you know the difference between the two.

- The two leading parties in the coalition government, the Centre Party and SDP, fell out with each other. Hermann Muller, the leader of the SDP, refused to agree to cuts in unemployment benefit, favoured by Heinrich Bruning, the leader of the Centre Party. Muller resigned, leaving Bruning as Chancellor, but without a majority in the *Reichstag*. Bruning asked President Hindenburg to use Article 48 of the Constitution which meant, in an emergency such as the depression, laws could be issued without having to go through the *Reichstag*.
- From 1930, Germany effectively ceased to be a democracy, as the *Reichstag* met less and less frequently, and it was seen as ineffective by many Germans. Moreover, the German government was now controlled by an 84-year-old President, an ex-army leader, who seemed well past his prime.
- To make matters worse, Bruning's government introduced unpopular economic policies to try to deal with the depression. They remembered the hyperinflation of 1923 and refused to increase government spending or print more money. Instead, the Chancellor raised taxes, which infuriated businessmen already suffering from the depression, reduced wages and made cuts in unemployment benefit.
- Many Germans now turned to support the more extreme parties, such as the communists and the Nazis, who seemed to offer possible solutions to the depression. The communists blamed the capitalist system and insisted that only a communist government could get Germany out of the depression. The Nazis, on the other hand, gave people scapegoats for Germany's economic problems – the Jews, the Weimar politicians and the communists.

Why was there increased support for the Nazi Party, 1929–1932?

The Nazi Party exploited the economic and political problems of the Weimar Republic through skilful propaganda, the appeal of Hitler and the activities of the SA.

The appeal of Hitler

Hitler did much to win support for the Nazi Party. Posters and rallies built him up as a 'superman'. He wore spectacles to read, but refused to be seen wearing them in public because he thought they were a sign of weakness. The campaigns focused around his personality and his skills, especially as a speaker. Hitler realised the need to focus on the main issues and provide the German people with a scapegoat. Many Germans had lost their jobs in the economic crisis. Hitler blamed the Weimar Republic and insisted that he was Germany's last hope. He promised to unite all Germans and make Germany rich and strong again.

He revived the 'stab in the back' theory, blaming Jews, communists and politicians for the German surrender and for signing the hated Treaty of Versailles. He promised revenge and the destruction of the Treaty of Versailles. Hitler accused the Jews of being responsible for all of Germany's problems and promised to get rid of them. In this way, he provided the Germans with someone to blame.

Source A: Otto Strasser, a Nazi who often opposed Hitler, wrote about his qualities as a speaker.

> 'As the spirit moves him, he is promptly transformed into one of the greatest speakers of the century. Adolf Hitler enters a hall. He sniffs the air. For a minute he gropes, feels his way, senses the atmosphere. Suddenly he bursts forth. His words go like an arrow to their target. He touches each private world in the raw, telling each person what they most want to hear.'

In addition the Nazis were very flexible in their approach. If they found that an idea was losing support, they would change it. If all else failed, Hitler made vague promises, such as they would 'make Germany great again'.

The work of the SA

The SA also played an important role in increasing support for the Nazi Party in a positive and negative way.

Positive

- By 1932, the SA numbered 600,000. The movement attracted many unemployed and unhappy young people who admired the discipline and fighting qualities of the Brownshirts.
- The SA organised parades through towns and cities, which impressed many Germans who saw order and discipline in a time of chaos.

Negative

- The SA was also used to intimidate any opposition. They frequently attacked and disrupted the meetings of rival groups, especially those of the Communist Party. They were often seen as bullies, something that worried respectable German voters. At times the SA acted independently of Hitler.

Activities

1 What can you learn from Source A about Hitler's strengths as a speaker?
2 Give examples of three of each of the following:
   - groups Hitler blamed
   - promises Hitler made.
3 Give two reasons why the SA won support for the Nazis.

Goebbels and Nazi propaganda

Goebbels was a master of the art of propaganda and used every possible method to get the Nazi message across. Many of his methods were ahead of his time.

Activities

4 Explain why propaganda was so important in increasing support for the Nazis in the years 1929–1932.

Posters

Posters targeted different audiences and were timed to have maximum impact. Their message was generally simple but clear.

Parades and marches

These were organised by mobile units to carry the message to every town and city in Germany, and were on a smaller scale than the Nazi rallies. They organised entertainment and speeches in different areas. They spent days winning over people with plays, concerts and sporting events.

Propaganda methods

Newspapers

The Nazis owned eight newspapers, such as *Der Stürmer* and *Völkischer Beobachter*, but were also given access to the media empire of Alfred Hugenburg. Each newspaper had its own character and was designed to appeal to its own readership.

Rallies

Rallies were on a huge scale with thousands of uniformed Nazis parading in massed ranks. The Nazis gave the impression of order and discipline. Nazi rallies consisted of Hitler giving a commanding speech in front of thousands of spectators. Goebbels took advantage of air flight and chartered planes to fly Hitler all over Germany in order to speak at four or five rallies per day. The campaign was given the name 'Hitler over Germany'.

Who supported the Nazis?

Hitler found something to appeal to all sections of German society. One historian has argued that Hitler won support because of 'negative cohesion'.

In other words, people were not attracted by Nazi ideas and promises, but shared Nazi fears and dislikes, for example of communism.

The countryside

It was in the rural areas of Germany that Nazism first became popular in the 1920s. Agricultural prices slumped even further after the Wall Street Crash. The Nazis promised to defend farmers' lands from the collectivisation of the communists.

The middle classes

The middle classes of shopkeepers, civil servants, professionals and teachers were afraid of communism on the one side and big business or capitalism on the other. The Nazis promised to protect them from both. They were also alarmed at increasing disorder and violence and were impressed by the discipline of the SA.

The upper classes

These were wealthy landowners or business people who felt especially threatened by the possibility of a communist takeover. The Nazis, with their promises to destroy communism and support big business, were the lesser of two evils. As early as 1929 Alfred Hugenburg, leader of the German Nationalist Party and a wealthy newspaper owner, worked with Hitler in attacking the Young Plan. He gave the Nazis access to his media empire, especially his cinemas. Big business gave funds to support the Nazi Party.

The working classes

Workers in the cities did not vote for the Nazis in large numbers, preferring the communists. However, outside the big cities most workers worked for small family firms. They did not belong to unions and were attracted by Hitler's promises of more rights for working people and better jobs.

40

Women

Hitler was very keen to win the votes of women and they were especially targeted in Nazi poster campaigns. He promised to make the family more important and give women a special place in their role as mothers and wives.

The young

Many strong supporters were young people. Over 40 per cent of those that joined before 1933 had been born between 1904 and 1913. They were attracted by Nazi ideals, the discipline of the SA and the promise of employment.

Activities

5 'Negative cohesion' was the main reason for increased Nazi support in the years 1929–1932.' From the evidence, how far do you agree or disagree with this view?

In your answer:

- Explain the meaning of 'negative cohesion' and give examples.

- Describe positive reasons for support for the Nazi Party.

- Decide to what extent you agree or disagree with this statement, and explain why.

6 'If Nazi Party support was a mile wide, it was at critical points an inch thick.' Discuss.

Summary

- There was little support for the Nazi Party in the years 1924–1929. Nevertheless, Hitler reorganised the Party to make it more effective in fighting for seats in the *Reichstag*.

- The depression that began in 1929 brought high unemployment and increasing dissatisfaction with the Weimar Republic.

- Hitler and the Nazis won support because of Hitler's personal appeal and clever use of propaganda.

- The Nazis were supported by several groups, especially big business (which feared a communist takeover).

41

1924
Hitler released from prison

1928
Nazis win twelve seats in *Reichstag* elections

1929
Wall Street Crash

1930
Nazis win 107 seats in *Reichstag* elections

1932
Nazis become the largest party in the *Reichstag*

Unemployment reaches 6 million

1933
January: Hitler becomes Chancellor of Germany

Quick quiz

1 Are the following statements true or false? If they are false, what is the correct answer?

	True or false	Correct answer
The Spartacists were led by Karl Liebknecht and Rosa Luxemburg		
The Kapp Putsch failed because of the actions of the German army		
The 'stab in the back' theory suggested that Germany had lost the war		
The French occupied the Ruhr because Germany failed to make its reparations payments		
Everyone in Germany was badly affected by hyperinflation		
Hitler joined the German Workers' Party in 1919		
The SA were known as the blackshirts		
The emblem of the Nazi Party was the swastika		
Passive resistance meant refusing to cooperate with the French		
German reparations payments were fixed at £3,300 million		

2 The following paragraph is not an accurate account of the period of recovery in the years 1924–1929.

(i) Find the errors.

(ii) Replace them with the correct answer.

Gustav Stresemann was Chancellor of Germany throughout the years 1924 to 1929. He negotiated the Dawes Plan with Britain, by which German reparations payments were increased. In addition, Britain agreed to give loans to Germany. In 1925, Stresemann took Germany out of the League of Nations. In 1926, Germany signed the Locarno Treaties with neighbouring countries such as Belgium, Holland and France. Finally, in 1929, Stresemann negotiated the Young Plan with France. This further increased German reparations payments.

3 Match the following definitions to the words and phrases:

Words/phrases	Definitions
Reparations	German parliament
Reichstag	Money loses all value as prices soar
SA	German name for being forced to sign the peace treaty
Hyperinflation	Stormtroopers
The diktat	My Struggle – Hitler's autobiography
Polish Corridor	Parties given seats in parliament in proportion to number of votes
Mein Kampf	Area which split Germany into two
Proportional representation	Compensation for war damage

Checklist

How well do you know and understand?

- The early problems of the Weimar Republic.
- The reasons for early opposition to the Republic.
- How successful the Republic was in dealing with these problems and the opposition.
- The causes and effects of the hyperinflation of 1923.
- The importance of the Munich *Putsch* of 1923.
- How far the Weimar Republic recovered in the years 1924–1929.
- Which groups supported the Nazi Party in the years 1921–1928.
- Why there was greater support for the Nazis in the years 1929–1932.
- Which groups supported the Nazis in the years 1929–1932.

Student tip

You need to have a very clear understanding of the chronology of the Weimar Republic, 1919–1932, to avoid confusing key events such as the hyperinflation of 1923 and the depression of 1929.

Plenary activities

Have you heard of a 'scatter graph'? This is often used to plot two sets of data and compare them. Here is an example of such a graph.

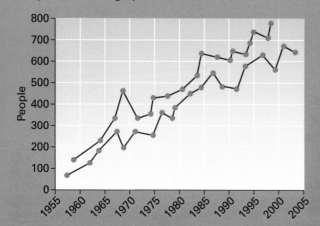

Make a copy of the following scatter graph.

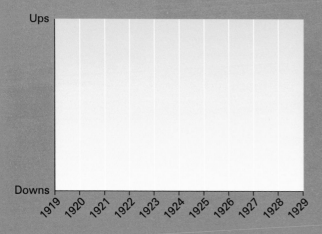

1 In the following table are key developments in the Weimar Republic and Nazi Party.
   - Find the key dates for each event.
   - Plot each development above the appropriate year on your graph. If you think it was very beneficial then put it near the top ('Ups'). If you think it was disastrous then put it near the bottom ('Downs').
   - Plot the developments in the Weimar Republic in blue on your graph.
   - Plot developments in the Nazi Party in red.

2 Are there any patterns or links in your graph? Explain your answer.

Weimar Republic	Nazi Party
Dawes Plan	Hitler in prison
Hyperinflation	1928 election result
Spartacists	Hitler joins the German Workers Party
Rentenmark	
Treaty of Versailles	Munich *Putsch*
French occupation of the Ruhr	Nazi Party set up
	Beginning of SA
Kapp *Putsch*	Hitler reorganises the Nazi Party
Entry to League of Nations	
	Reorganisation of Nazi Party

Government of the Third Reich to 1945

Introduction

In the 18 months after Hitler became Chancellor, the Nazis were able to establish a dictatorship of the Nazi Party. Potential opposition groups, such as communists and trades unionists, were removed as Germany became a one-party state. However, the greatest threat came from within the Nazi Party, from Röhm and the SA leaders, who were eventually purged on the Night of the Long Knives.

The Nazis had two methods for ensuring support for their regime: terror and persuasion. Terror was achieved through the establishment of a police state run by the feared SS and the secret police, the *Gestapo*. Many opponents of the Nazi regime were arrested and sent to concentration camps. Persuasion was achieved through propaganda. Goebbels carefully manipulated every possible opportunity to pass on Nazi ideals, including the radio and the cinema.

There was some opposition to the Nazi government, especially from teenage rebels such as the Edelweiss Pirates, who refused to conform to the Nazi views on the role of the young. Church leaders, such as Martin Niemöller, also publicly expressed their opposition to Nazi ideas. All opposition was ruthlessly repressed.

A photomontage from 1932 by John Heartfield.

A painting by Paul Padua entitled The *Führer* Speaks (1937).

Aims and outcomes

By the end of this section, you should be able to understand, explain and describe...

- how Hitler established a dictatorship of the Nazi Party in the years 1933–1934
- the key features of the police state
- the importance of propaganda in Nazi Germany
- the opposition and resistance to the Third *Reich*.

This photograph shows the public hanging of a group of resistance fighters, some of whom were from the 'Edelweiss Pirates'.

1933

February: *Reichstag* Fire.
March: The Enabling Law
June: All rival political parties banned.

A fresco by the Mexican artist Diego Rivera, 1933.

Activities

1 What is the message in the joke in the Fascinating fact box?

2 Study any of the three small illustrations on the opposite page. Put together a text that you would send to a friend describing the scene in each one. (You are limited to 160 characters.)

3 Study the fresco on this page. Is the artist a supporter or opponent of the Nazis? Give examples from the fresco to explain your answer.

FASCINATING FACT

Ludwig Schroer, who owned a confectionery shop, was arrested for telling jokes about Hitler. He was sent to Buchenwald concentration camp. He later hanged himself to escape a second term in Buchenwald. Here is an example of a joke by the Munich cabaret artist Weiss-Ferdl, the sort of thing that led to Shroer's arrest: *'My friend Adolf has given me his picture and he has even signed it! Now I've got a problem – shall I hang him, or shall I put him up against a wall?'*

1934
June: Night of the Long Knives. Leaders of the SA purged.
August: Death of President Hindenburg. Hitler becomes *Führer*.

1936
Berlin Olympics.

1937
Arrest of Martin Niemöller.

1939
3 September: Start of the Second World War.

1944
'July Plot' fails to assassinate Hitler.

1945
7 May: End of Second World War in Europe.

2.1 Creation of the Nazi state

Learning outcomes

By the end of this topic you should be able to:

- understand the reasons why Hitler was invited to become Chancellor in January 1933
- explain the methods he used to remove opposition in the years 1933–1934
- describe Hitler's role as *Führer*.

Getting an overview

Shown here are the steps by which Hitler created the **Third Reich** and made himself dictator of Germany. Begin with the bottom step and read upwards.

Democracy: Where people choose the government from two or more parties at an election

Dictatorship: One-party state governed by one person who has total control

Führer: German for leader

Purge: To remove enemies by terror

State parliament: Each German state, such as Bavaria and Saxony, elected its own parliament

The SS: The *Schutzstaffel* ('Elite Guard') were set up as Hitler's private bodyguard, but grew to control many aspects of life in the Third Reich, from the police to the economy to the death camps

Third Reich: Third empire

The steps to dictatorship, 1932–1934

Hitler becomes *Führer*
Within hours of Hindenburg's death, Hitler had declared himself '*Führer* and *Reich* Chancellor'.

Death of Hindenburg
In August 1934 Hindenburg died.

Night of the Long Knives
Hitler's position was threatened by Röhm, the leader of the SA, who wanted to merge with the army. Hitler did not want to upset powerful army leaders. In June 1934, on the Night of the Long Knives, Röhm and other SA leaders were murdered by the SS.

Removal of power groups
Between May and June 1933 rival power groups were removed. Trade Union leaders were arrested and the unions were merged into the German Labour Front. The offices of political parties such as the Social Democrats, were occupied and their newspapers and funds confiscated. By July 1933 Germany was a one-party state.

The Enabling Act
This was passed in March 1933 and gave Hitler the power to pass laws without the consent of the *Reichstag*.

The *Reichstag* Fire
In February 1933 the *Reichstag* building was set on fire. A Dutch communist, Marius van der Lubbe, was accused of the crime. This gave Hitler the excuse to ban his greatest rivals, the Communist Party.

Becoming Chancellor
From 1930 Hindenburg used his emergency powers to rule without the *Reichstag* and, in 1932, Germany had three chancellors, including Franz von Papen. Eventually, however, Hindenburg had little choice but to choose Hitler as Chancellor, on 30 January 1933, as the Nazis were the largest party in the *Reichstag*.

Source A: Extract from Goebbels' diary, 8 December 1932.

'Severe depression prevails. Financial worries make all systematic work impossible. The danger now exists of the whole Party going to pieces. Dr Ley phones that the situation in the Party is becoming more critical from hour to hour. For hours on end the *Führer* walks anxiously up and down the hotel room. Once he stops, he says "If the Party should ever break up, I'll make an end of things in three minutes with a revolver."'

Source B: A photomontage from September 1932, by John Heartfield, an opponent of Hitler and the Nazis. The slogan reads: 'Millions stand behind me'.

Activities

1 Study the illustration, 'The steps to dictatorship, 1932–1934' on the opposite page. Make your own steps using a maximum of five words to summarise the key features of each step.

2 Which do you think was the most important step? Give reasons for your choice.

3 What can you learn from Source A about the Nazi Party in November 1932?

4 Study Source B. What is the message of the photomontage?

examzone
Top tip!

For answers on the rise of Hitler and the Nazi Party make sure that you place it in the context of events at the time. Think about not only the policies of the party or appeal to different groups, but also the impact of the depression on the German people.

MILLIONEN
stehen hinter mir

Why did Hitler become Chancellor in January 1933?

In the years 1929-1932, more and more Germans supported extremist parties because they felt the Weimar government was failing to act decisively. The way the government had been set up was part of the problem (see page 10). It meant that parties such as the Nazis could gain *Reichstag* seats without huge numbers of votes.

With so many different parties in the *Reichstag*, there was a lot of disagreement. This made it difficult for the Chancellor to act decisively. To pass laws he needed a majority in the *Reichstag*, which was hard to get. Too often the Chancellor had to get the President to rule by decree, making it look as if the government was failing.

Date	Key event	Key features
March 1932	The Presidential elections	In the election for President, Hitler fought against Hindenburg. Although Hindenburg won with 19.4 million votes, Hitler's reputation improved because he received 13.4 million votes.
May 1932	The fall of Bruning	Bruning had lost popularity in the years 1930–1932 because he had reduced unemployment benefit and increased taxes. Moreover, he did not have a majority in the *Reichstag* so was dependent on Hindenburg's decree. Following the advice of a senior army officer, General von Schleicher, Hindenburg removed Bruning.
May 1932	The Papen government	Von Papen, a friend of Hindenburg, was appointed Chancellor. He was leader of the Centre Party, but had only 68 supporters in the *Reichstag* and was dependent on government by decree.
July 1932	Elections	Von Papen held elections hoping to gain more support. The elections, however, were a great success for the Nazis, who won 230 seats and became the largest party in the *Reichstag*. Hitler demanded the post of Chancellor. Hindenburg, who disliked Hitler, refused to appoint him. Hindenburg mistrusted Hitler and believed that the Nazis were too violent to be given power. Furthermore, Hitler had only been a corporal in the First World War while Hindenburg had been a Field Marshall. Instead, Hindenburg asked von Papen to remain in office.
July–November 1932	The Papen government	The new *Reichstag* did not support von Papen and in September 1932 his government lost a vote of no confidence by 512 votes to 42, which led to the November 1932 election. Until that time, von Papen was again dependent on the presidential decree and the support of Hindenburg.
November 1932	Elections	Von Papen arranged another election for the *Reichstag*, hoping to win more support. This time he won even fewer seats, though the Nazis' seats also fell to 196. This was partly due to a shortage of funds for the election campaign, as they had already fought two other campaigns in 1932. Some Germans were also alarmed at the increasing violence of the SA. Von Papen asked Hindenburg to close down the *Reichstag* and rule by decree.

Date	Key event	Key features
December 1932 to January 1933	Schleicher government	Von Schleicher warned Hindenburg that a von Papen government would lead to civil war and even more violence from the Nazis and communists. Hindenburg therefore appointed von Schleicher as Chancellor; he lasted less than two months.
January 1933	Von Papen, Hitler and Hindenburg	Von Papen was furious with von Schleicher and, behind the scenes, began to negotiate with Hitler to make him Chancellor, with himself as Vice-Chancellor. Hindenburg still refused to accept a Nazi government.
28 January 1933	Von Schleicher resigns	Von Schleicher failed to win support in the *Reichstag* and resigned as Chancellor. Von Papen persuaded Hindenburg to appoint Hitler as Chancellor, warning him that the alternative would be civil war. Hindenburg agreed, as long as there were only a few Nazis in the Cabinet. **Source C:** An account by the State Secretary in Hindenburg's office, given after the Second World War. 'Despite Papen's persuasions, Hindenburg was extremely hesitant, until the end of January, to make Hitler Chancellor. He wanted to have Papen again as Chancellor. Papen finally won him over to Hitler with the argument that, if the present opportunity was missed, a revolt of the National Socialists and civil war was likely.'
30 January 1933	Hitler becomes Chancellor	Hindenburg and von Papen were convinced that they would be able to use Hitler initially, and then get rid of him later.

Activities

1. Who was most responsible for bringing Hitler and the Nazis to power: Bruning, von Papen, von Schleicher or Hindenburg?

2. Make a copy of the following rating line and place each person somewhere on the line, giving a brief explanation for your decision.

←——————————————————→

Least responsible   Most responsible

3. 'Hitler came to power because he had the popular support of the German people.' Do you agree or disagree with this view?

   a) Examine the evidence of popular support for the Nazis.

   b) Examine the political developments from 1932 to January 1933.

   c) Make a final judgement on the question, giving your reasons.

examzone
Build better answers

Explain the importance of von Papen's role in Hitler's rise to power. (9 marks)

■ **Basic, Level 1**
Answer makes undeveloped statements without details, for example: *he persuaded people to appoint Hitler.*

● **Good, Level 2**
Answer adds detail to describe von Papen's actions.

▲ **Excellent, Level 3**
Answer explains the significance of von Papen's role – showing, with details, that his persuasion was crucial in overcoming Hindenburg's objections to the appointment of Hitler as Chancellor.

How did Hitler remove opposition in the years 1933–1934?

Within 18 months of achieving power, Hitler had removed the major threats to the Nazi regime.

The *Reichstag* Fire, February 1933

On 27 February 1933, the *Reichstag* building was burned down. Inside the building the Berlin police found a Dutch communist, Marius van der Lubbe, who was arrested, put on trial and found guilty of starting the fire. Hitler was able to take advantage of this to accuse the German Communist Party of plotting to take over the government. Four thousand communists were arrested on the night of the fire. The day after, Hitler was able to persuade Hindenburg to pass an emergency decree giving the police the powers to search houses, confiscate property and detain people without trial.

Activities

1 Write a newspaper headline for a Nazi newspaper the day after the *Reichstag* Fire.

2 Write down two reasons that blame the communists for the *Reichstag* Fire, and two that blame the Nazis.

Source A: Van der Lubbe in a statement to the police.

'As to the question whether I acted alone, I declare absolutely that this was the case. No one helped me at all.'

Source B: From a British journalist.

'Five minutes after the fire had broken out I was outside the *Reichstag* watching the flames licking their way up the great dome into the tower. After about twenty minutes I suddenly saw the famous black car of Adolf Hitler slide past. I rushed over just as Göring joined him in the lobby. "This is undoubtedly the work of the communists, Herr Chancellor," he said. "A number of communist deputies were present here in the *Reichstag* twenty minutes before the fire broke out. We have succeeded in arresting one of the arsonists."'

The police were now able to target the Communist Party leaders.

There have been many theories about what caused the fire. Was it the work of the communists or did the Nazis themselves start it?

Were the communists to blame?
Van der Lubbe was caught red handed and confessed to the crime.

Source C: From Göring's testimony at van der Lubbe's trial (Göring was Minister of the Interior).

'It never occurred to me that the Reichstag might have been set on fire. I thought the fire had been caused by carelessness. In this moment I knew that the Communist Party was the culprit. I only wish that the rest of the world had seen it so clearly.'

The election of March 1933

The election results of March 1933 gave the Nazis more seats than ever before. However, they still had fewer than half the total. The communists had 81 seats and, in order to change the German constitution, Hitler needed a two-thirds majority.

Source E: The election results of March 1933.

	Seats
The Nazis	288
Social Democratic Party	120
Communist Party	81
Centre Party	74
Nationalist Party	52
Other parties	32

Were the Nazis to blame?
The fire seemed too much of a coincidence, in that it gave Hitler the ideal excuse to remove the communist threat.

Source F: From a letter written by a British journalist who witnessed the fire.

'That evening Hitler himself was not absolutely certain that the fire was a communist plot. As we walked side by side through the burning building he said, "God grant that this be the work of the communists."'

Source G: From a modern world history text written in 2001.

'It could well have been the Nazis who set fire to the building and then framed van der Lubbe in order to provide an excuse to persecute the communists. The fire came at a very convenient time for Hitler, just before the March elections. Moreover, the Nazis hated the *Reichstag* which was seen as a symbol of the Weimar Republic.'

Source D: General Halder remembers a conversation with Hitler.

'At a luncheon on the birthday of the *Führer* in 1942 the conversation turned to the *Reichstag* Fire. I heard with my own ears when Göring interrupted the conversation and shouted: "The only one who really knows about the *Reichstag* building is I, because I set it on fire."'

Source H: A Nazi poster used during the March election campaign. The poster reads: 'President Hindenburg and Hitler asking the voters "to fight with us for peace and equal rights".'

DER MARSCHALL UND DER GEFREITE

KÄMPFEN MIT UNS FÜR FRIEDEN UND GLEICHBERECHTIGUNG

How did Hitler remove rival groups?

The Enabling Act

Hitler now wanted the *Reichstag* to pass an 'Enabling Act' which would give him the power for the next four years to make laws without the consent of the *Reichstag*. He achieved the necessary two-thirds majority by using the emergency decree to prevent the Communist Party from taking up the 81 seats they had won. He retained the support of the Nationalist Party, which had 52 seats. In addition, he gained the support of the Centre Party, which had 74 seats, by promising to defend the interests of the Catholic Church.

The Enabling Act was passed by 444 votes to 94, with the SA surrounding the *Reichstag* building to ensure that the majority was achieved. Hitler now had the powers of a dictator and Germany ceased to be a **democracy**.

Source A: The Enabling Act.

Article 1	The *Reich* Cabinet is authorised to enact laws.
Article 2	The laws enacted by the *Reich* Cabinet may deviate from the Constitution.
Article 3	The laws enacted by the *Reich* Cabinet shall be prepared by the Chancellor.
Article 5	The law comes into effect on the day of its publication. It ceases to be valid on 1 April 1937.

Source B: The front page of a book, *A People in Chains*, written by an exiled opponent of the Nazi regime in 1934.

Using the powers now given to him by the Enabling Act, Hitler removed further opposition to the Nazi government.

State parliaments [cancelled]

Germany was a federation of eighteen states, each with its own parliament, police and laws. On 31 March 1933, the Nazis closed down all **state parliaments**. They were then reorganised so that the Nazis had a majority in each state parliament. Hitler also appointed Nazi state governors, who had the power to appoint and dismiss state officials and make state laws. In January 1934 Hitler abolished all state parliaments and made all state governments subordinate to central government.

Trade Unions [cancelled]

These were a threat because they could organise strikes against the Nazi regime. In addition, members might see their first allegiance as being to the union rather than the Nazi Party. Moreover, many union leaders had close links to the rival Communist and Socialist Parties. Furthermore, their removal would please employers and businessmen. On 2 May 1933 Nazis broke into trade union offices all over Germany and arrested many trade union officials. The unions were then merged into a 'German Labour Front'.

Rival political parties [cancelled]

Hitler wanted a one-party state in which all Germans supported the Nazi Party. On 10 May 1933 the Nazis occupied the offices of the Social Democrat Party and destroyed its newspapers and confiscated its funds. Two weeks later the Communist Party suffered the same fate. In July 1933 Hitler introduced a law stating that the Nazi Party was the only party allowed in Germany.

Activities

1. In pairs, examine the evidence about the *Reichstag* Fire. Who do you think started the fire?
2. Do you think it is impossible to *prove* who started the fire? Explain the reasons for your answer.
3. Study Source A. How important was the Enabling Act in removing opposition to the Nazi regime? Explain your answer.
4. Study Source B. To what extent do you agree that the German people were 'a people in chains' by 1934?

The Night of the Long Knives, June 1934

The final threat to Hitler came, surprisingly, from within his own party: from Röhm and the SA. This threat was removed when the SA was purged, on what became known as the 'Night of the Long Knives'.

Why was the SA purged?

The SA was purged for several reasons. Röhm, as leader of the SA, was a genuine threat to Hitler's own position as leader. Röhm was the commander of a very large organisation of nearly 2 million men, whose members were increasingly violent and out of control at a time when Hitler was trying to establish, through legal methods, a **dictatorship**.

A photograph of Ernst Röhm, leader of the SA.

Moreover, Röhm wanted to merge the SA with the German army. Hitler realised that this 'second revolution' would alienate army leaders, who were still powerful enough to threaten the foundations of the Nazi regime. In addition, Röhm favoured a second revolution, which would lead to more socialist policies. This worried many industrialists who were important supporters of the Nazi Party.

Source C: From comments by Röhm made in a private conversation with a Nazi friend.

> 'Adolf is a swine. He is betraying all of us. He is getting matey with the Prussian generals. Adolf knows exactly what I want. I've told him often enough. The generals are a lot of old fogeys. I'm the nucleus of the new army, don't you see that? Hitler puts me off with fair words.'

The **purge** was also the outcome of a power struggle between leading Nazis. Heinrich Himmler, leader of **the SS**, wanted his organisation to supersede that of the SA. Hermann Göring, the Minister of the Interior, also favoured the removal of Röhm and his increasingly violent SA. Finally, Röhm's own homosexual preferences had done much to tarnish the image of the Nazi Party.

Source D: From a letter written by the Minister of the Interior in October 1933.

> 'New infringements by the SA have been reported again and again during the past few weeks. Above all, SA leaders and men have carried out police actions for which they have no authority. The infringements and excesses must now cease once and for all.'

What happened on the Night of the Long Knives?

Hitler arranged a meeting with Röhm and 100 other SA leaders at a hotel in the Bavarian resort of Bad Wiessee on the evening of 30 June 1934. The SA leaders were arrested by heavily armed members of the SS and taken to Munich where they were shot.

Over the next few days, various individuals who were seen as threats to Hitler's position were purged, including Gregor Strasser and General von Schleicher. Hitler used the excuse that Röhm and the SA were planning a revolution to take over the government.

Source E: Report of a press conference given by Göring on 2 July 1934.

> 'General Göring explained that he and Herr Himmler, who was responsible for security, had been watching for weeks, even months and had been aware that preparations for a "second revolution" were being made by certain ambitious SA leaders, headed by Röhm. Hitler had decided to suppress the movement with a firm hand at a suitable moment.'

Source F: From a history written in 1971.

> 'The smoothness with which the murders of 30 June were carried out is powerful proof that no Röhm plot was imminent. There was no resistance encountered anywhere… Many victims unsuspectingly surrendered voluntarily, believing it was all a big mistake. The only shots fired were those of the executioners… The numbers of victims is estimated at between 150 and 200.'

What were the results of the purge?

The purge enabled Hitler to remove possible rivals to his position, especially Strasser and Röhm, and ensured the continued support of army leaders. Furthermore, he now established the SS as a separate organisation from the SA, with Himmler taking orders directly from Hitler. The SA was now firmly under Hitler's control.

The death of Hindenburg

On 2 August 1934, Hindenburg died. He had still held presidential powers, so had been the only obstacle to Hitler's total control. The day he died, Hitler acted swiftly. He said that he would now rule Germany with the powers of Chancellor and President, as *Führer*. Now no-one could hold him back.

The army oath of allegiance

On the very same day, Hitler also announced that the army's oath of allegiance was to be sworn to him personally, not to Germany. If it came to a power struggle, it was his orders they had sworn to obey – not those of any military leader or any other member of government. A public vote was held to confirm Hitler as *Führer* – he got 90 per cent of the vote.

Source G: A cartoon from a British newspaper, 3 July 1934.

Hitler as *Führer*

Hitler was, in some ways, a lazy ruler. He suffered from insomnia and did not go to bed until 2.00 or 3.00 am. He often slept in till late morning, did not get involved in lengthy meetings or discussions with leading Nazis and left the details of government to others.

There were few challenges to his leadership, and he often played off one leading Nazi against another to avoid any possible threats. He would issue edicts to make changes in the law.

Activities

5 What reasons are given in Sources C and D on page 53 for the purges?

6 Study Source G on the opposite page. What is the message of the cartoon?

7 'The SA posed the greatest threat to Hitler in the years 1933–1934'. How far do you agree or disagree with this view? You may use the following in your answer and any other information of your own:

- Röhm and the SA
- The communists
- Hindenburg.

The cult of the *Führer*

Hitler had a very personal system of government, based upon his own popularity, or 'the cult of the *Führer*'. To millions of Germans in the 1930s, Hitler was more than just a leader. He was the law-giver and almost a god-like leader.

1932
Germany has three chancellors – Bruning, Papen and Schleicher

1933
Hitler becomes Chancellor of Germany
Reichstag Fire
Enabling Law passed

1934
Night of the Long Knives
The death of Hindenburg

Heil Hitler
All public employees had to greet others with the 'German salute' while saying 'Heil Hitler'.

Unmarried
Hitler didn't marry until the end of his life. He was portrayed as a man who had sacrificed personal happiness to serve his country.

An official portrait of Hitler, 1937.

Image
Hitler was presented as an ordinary soldier who had emerged as the creator of a new Germany.

Man of the people
Photographs were issued to show him as an ordinary person, a man of the people. He was seen relaxing, playing with his dogs or simply reading the newspaper. As he toured the country people got the chance to meet him.

Summary

- The *Reichstag* Fire gave Hitler and the Nazis the ideal excuse to remove the communist threat.
- The legal basis of Hitler's dictatorship was the Enabling Act of March 1933. Within a few months he had created a one-party state.
- Röhm and the SA threatened Hitler's position as leader and the continued support of the army. This threat was removed on the Night of the Long Knives.
- With the death of Hindenburg, Hitler became *Führer* and the Nazis carefully developed the 'Hitler myth'.

2.2 Nazi methods of control

Learning outcomes

By the end of this topic you should be able to:

- understand the meaning of the Nazi police state
- explain censorship and propaganda under the Nazis
- describe Nazi policies towards the Churches.

Getting an overview

The Nazis used two very different methods to control the German people: fear and **indoctrination**.

Aryan: Nazi term used to describe people of 'pure' German blood with no ancestors from races they saw as 'inferior', such as Poles, Slavs or Jews. The Nazis' ideal Aryan was white-skinned, blue-eyed, and blonde

Censorship: When unacceptable parts, or whole books, films, etc., are officially suppressed

Concentration camps: Prisons where inmates were treated with great brutality

Concordat: Agreement

Gestapo: Nazi secret police

Indoctrination: Brainwashing people into accepting ideas

Police state: A totalitarian state controlled by a police force

By fear

The police state

German people would be too frightened to oppose the state because:

- the police had far-reaching powers
- the *Gestapo* (or secret police) was used to hunt out opponents of the Nazis
- the *Gestapo* was helped by the SS
- opponents were sent to concentration camps.

Law courts

The legal system was controlled by the Nazis:

- there was no trial by jury
- all judges were Nazis.

The Churches

The Catholic and Protestant Churches were seen as a threat because the beliefs of Christianity were very different from Nazi beliefs:

- a Nazi Reich Church was set up with the intention of eventually replacing the Protestant Church
- there were some attempts to co-operate with the Catholic Church; however, the closures of Catholic schools and youth movements led to opposition from some priests, and their later arrest.

By indoctrination

Censorship

- The media, culture, music, art, and even architecture, were carefully controlled by the Ministry of Propaganda and Enlightenment to ensure that they put forward Nazi ideas
- large numbers of books were burned to get rid of any books by Jews and communists.

Propaganda

Josef Goebbels was Minister of Propaganda and he used many different methods to convert the German people to Nazi ideas. These included:

- cheap radios to ensure that most Germans could hear Nazi broadcasts
- use of films to put across the Nazi message
- rallies such as Nuremberg to show the power of the Nazis
- posters to put across important ideas.

Source A: A Nazi poster that reads: 'All Germany hears the *Führer*'. Hitler wanted to create the 'Thousand Year *Reich*', and wanted people to genuinely believe in and support Nazi ideas.

The police state

A police state is one where the government uses the police to control the population. Often, it uses ordinary police and secret police, who have absolute power of arrest. The most powerful of all the police in the Nazi state, the SS, were neither secret nor ordinary. Their leader was Heinrich Himmler.

Himmler

Himmler took over the SS in 1929. He was totally loyal to Hitler, saying that it did not matter if his work broke 'some clause in the law' because he was acting for the *Führer* and for Germany. He increased the numbers of the SS, only recruiting men of **Aryan** appearance (strong, blue-eyed, fair-haired). In 1932 he introduced a black uniform with silver 'lightning flashes' (resembling 'S's) as a badge, making them instantly recognisable from other members of the army or police.

The SS

The SS had begun as Hitler's personal bodyguard of eight men. Under Himmler the SS expanded to hundreds of thousands and it was given control over all other branches of the police in Germany. It was SS officers who were in charge of the killings during the Night of the Long Knives. The SS could arrest whoever they wanted and imprison them without trial. The SS ran the **concentration camps**, which were used to hold political prisoners and 'undesirable' people the Nazis wanted out of Germany. When the Nazis began to use death camps to murder people, the SS ran those too.

Always watching

The *Gestapo* (secret police) worked under the SS. They spied on people and used a system of informants that meant that people soon knew there were spies everywhere ready to inform on them. Phones were regularly tapped and the

Gestapo could enter anyone's home without a search warrant. The *Gestapo* also gave local 'block wardens' the right to go and ask questions in the homes of their 'block'. People were expected to co-operate with the block wardens, and let them into their homes on demand.

Source A: A description by an American visitor to Germany in 1939.

'The National Socialist Secret Police made silent arrests. Late at night and early in the morning they took man after man. As accurately as I could learn, this is how the arrests were made. The door bell or door knocker sounded. There stood two, or at most three, tall men with pairs of pistols in their belts. The chosen hour was one at which they find the wanted man relaxed, surprising him at a meal or in bed.'

Source B: A photomontage by a well-known opponent of the Nazis. It has the title 'A letter from the *Gestapo*'. It refers to the method used by the *Gestapo* to inform relatives of a death by illness or 'while trying to escape' from a concentration camp.

57

Removing civil rights

The Nazis steadily passed laws to erode the civil rights of its citizens. The Decree for the Protection of People and State, passed in February 1933, gave the Nazis the right to restrict the civil rights of German citizens 'until further notice'. It was supposed to be an emergency measure, to root out communism after the Reichstag Fire, but it was never overturned. Political parties were banned. The Gestapo could arrest people for no reason and imprison them without trial. They could search homes without a warrant, tap phones and open letters. People could be imprisoned for no good reason and never get a fair trial. All judges had to swear an oath of loyalty to Hitler, so opponents of Hitler would not get a fair trial anyway. The SS, the Gestapo and even Hitler himself, often stepped in and changed sentences they disagreed with. The decree was used to remove other civil rights. For example, trade unions were banned and many of their leaders were arrested.

What were concentration camps?

The early concentration camps were disused factories or warehouses, but gradually the Nazi regime set up a national network of camps with the first one being opened at Dachau in 1933. These were used for questioning, torture and 're-education'. Prisoners were used as hard labour and treated with great brutality. Many died and their families were simply sent a note saying the victim had died of pneumonia or a similar disease.

Inmates in concentration camps wore badges, which indicated the reason for their imprisonment:

- Jews' badges were yellow
- religious groups, such as Catholics and Protestants, who opposed the Nazi regime wore purple badges
- those classed by the Nazis as mentally retarded or work-shy, including gypsies, vagabonds, tramps and alcoholics, wore black
- professional criminals wore green badges
- sexual offenders wore pink (the Nazis put homosexuals in this category)
- foreign forced-labour groups wore blue
- political prisoners (including communists, members of other political parties, and Trade Union leaders) wore a red triangle.

Source C: A survivor describes his experiences at Oranienburg concentration camp.

'I and three other leaders of the Socialist Workers' Party were ordered into the punishment stockade, a wooden structure 60 cm by 60 cm. You could only stand upright in it – you couldn't sit or even bend. I was in it for four days. I was beaten repeatedly in between. After four days my whole body was swollen from standing up.'

Source D: From a modern historian, written in 2000.

'Although the *Gestapo* was not as all-powerful as is often proclaimed, and evidence suggests considerable support for the regime, the brutality of the Third *Reich* must not be underestimated. Basic individual freedoms were removed in 1933. Thousands of Germans were rounded up into concentration camps, and those viewed as outsiders to their new society were imprisoned.'

Source E: From a modern historian, written in 2000.

'However, some historians now argue that [the Gestapo's] power rested on popular consent more than terror... Several major weaknesses have been seen in the *Gestapo* as a repressive body. Firstly, it lacked the personnel to effectively carry out central directives. Major areas such as Frankfurt, Hanover and Bremen had fewer than 50 officers each... At its peak, the *Gestapo* had only 30,000 officers for the whole country... Furthermore, most of these were office workers rather than field agents.'

Activities

1 How did the Nazis create a police state?
2 Explain the importance of the role of concentration camps in the police state.
3 What can you learn from Source B on page 57 about the *Gestapo*?
4 From the evidence of Sources D and E, did the Nazis create a 'ruthlessly efficient police state'?

Censorship and propaganda

Hitler was determined to control the German people through persuasion. **Censorship** and propaganda were used to ensure that people accepted and conformed to Nazi thinking.

Source A: Students taking part in book-burning in 1933.

Censorship

Once Hitler had become Chancellor, he appointed Goebbels as Minister of Enlightenment and Propaganda. This meant that Goebbels controlled the press, radio, publishing, films and the arts. The Nazis were determined to remove any alternative or rival ideas or beliefs.

59

Activities

1 Draw a sketch to show the meaning of censorship.
2 Identify two things that you can learn from Source A about Nazi censorship.
3 Give two examples of Nazi censorship.

A photograph of Josef Goebbels, Minister of Propaganda.

Books

No book could be published without Goebbels' permission.

Newspapers

Those that opposed Nazi views were closed down. The remaining newspapers had to get their news and their opinions from the Nazi news agency.

Book burning

Goebbels ordered the public burning of those books that disagreed with Nazi views.

Radio

The radio was controlled and all radios were designed to have a short range so they could not pick up foreign stations.

Reich Chamber of Culture

This was set up in 1938 to monitor cultural activities. Membership was only granted to those whose work was approved by the Nazis. Those denied membership found it impossible to get their work published or performed in Germany.

60

Propaganda

In the years after 1933, the Nazis made extensive use of propaganda in order to ensure that Hitler stayed in control. To the Nazis, everything had propaganda value.

Source B: Hitler writing in *Mein Kampf* in 1925.

> 'The purpose of propaganda is to convince the masses, whose slowness of understanding needs to be given time in order to absorb information. Only constant repetition will finally succeed in imprinting an idea on the mind.'

Posters

These had been successful in promoting Nazi ideals in the years before 1933, and were used extensively to put across the Nazi message and create the Hitler myth.

Source C: The poster says 'This hand leads the *Reich*. Young Germans follow it in the ranks'.

Radio

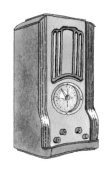

This was perhaps Goebbels' greatest success, because it offered the Nazis access to the homes of ordinary people. In March 1933, he told controllers of German radio: 'I consider radio to be the most crucial instrument that exists for influencing the masses.' He ordered the mass production of cheap radios so that by 1939 about 70 per cent of German homes had a radio. In addition, people were encouraged to listen to radio broadcasts in factories, bars and cafes. Loudspeakers were even erected in streets to relay important Nazi messages.

Cinema

Goebbels had a great interest in the cinema and appreciated its value as a method of putting across Nazi ideas. The Nazis produced about 1,300 films during their period in power. However, only about 200 were propaganda films. He realised that German people wanted to be entertained and would be bored with obvious propaganda films. High-quality films were produced with subtle Nazi messages about national sacrifice, the superiority of the Aryan race, anti-Semitism and the evils of communism. Cinemas were well attended and with every film there was shown a 45-minute newsreel about the success of the Nazis and their leader, Hitler.

Berlin Olympics 1936

This provided the ideal opportunity for the regime to advertise its successes. A vast new stadium that could hold 110,000 people was built. Filming of the event was under the direction of Leni Riefenstahl (a well-known German film director). Germany won far more medals than any other nation. This appeared to show the superiority of the Aryan race. However, one black athlete, Jesse Owens, won four gold medals and seemed to disprove Hitler's theory of Aryan superiority.

Rallies

Image was very important. People would believe that Hitler was making Germany great if they could see it. Goebbels organised mass rallies and marches that projected the image of power and terror. Every year a Party rally was held at Nuremberg.

Culture

The Nazis had strong objections to modern forms of culture. They despised modern art, progressive theatre and jazz music. They used all culture as a method of promoting their ideals. Artists were encouraged to use 'Aryan themes' such as the family, national community, and heroism.

Source D: A painting by Paul Padua in 1937 entitled *The Führer Speaks*.

Source E: Martha Brixius remembering life in Marburg in 1933.

'I was in Hanover on the day that Hitler's motorcade drove by. From an open car Hitler waved to wildly cheering crowds. I noticed how such a mass of enthusiastic people saluted and threw flowers that I was in danger of being pulled along. It infected you. And you think, could you be wrong and all the others right? I am also very much against the military but when I hear military music I get goose bumps.'

Activities

4   What examples of Nazi propaganda can you find in Source D?

5   What new methods were used by Goebbels to put across the Nazi message?

6   Which propaganda method do you think had the greatest impact on the German people?

   • Make a copy of the following line.

   • Plot each method on the line.

   • Give a brief explanation for each decision.

Least responsible ←————————→ Most responsible

Activities

7   What can you learn from Source E about the impact of propaganda on the German people?

8   Work in pairs for this activity. Which was more effective in ensuring support for the Nazi regime, fear or persuasion?

   • Evaluate the impact of fear – the police state.

   • Evaluate the impact of persuasion – propaganda and censorship.

   • Make a final judgement on their effectiveness, giving your reasons.

9   'The Nazis were effective in the use of propaganda.' Discuss.

The Churches

Hitler and the Nazis were opposed to the beliefs of the Christian Church. Whereas the Nazis believed in racial superiority, the dominance of the strong over the weak and the use of violence, Christianity believed in the strong helping the weak, love, forgiveness, respect and tolerance. In addition, the Christian belief in God was in conflict with the Nazi attempts to create the Hitler myth, the *Führer* as an almost God-like figure. Indeed, in the long term, Nazism would become the religion of the German people.

In Germany, about two-thirds of the people were Protestant and a third were Roman Catholics.

Nazism as a religion

This diagram demonstrates how the key features of Nazism could be compared with those found in religion.

God	
Symbol	
Disciples	
Bible	

The Catholic Church

Hitler was determined to reduce the influence of the Catholic Church for several reasons:

- Catholics owed their first allegiance to the Pope, a foreign leader, rather than to Hitler and the Nazi Party
- Catholics had consistently supported the Centre Party, a rival to the Nazis
- Catholic parents preferred to send their children to the Catholic youth movement rather than the Hitler Youth, where children were groomed to be loyal Nazis
- there were many Catholic schools where education was not subjected to the level of control and propaganda faced by children in schools run by the state.

At first Hitler decided to cooperate with the Catholic Church. Equally, the Catholic Church, especially the Pope, was keen to work with the Nazis, as they both hated communism. In 1933, Hitler signed an agreement known as a **Concordat**. Hitler promised not to interfere with the Catholic Church, which was guaranteed freedom to worship and run its own youth organisations and schools. In return, the Catholic Church agreed to stay out of politics.

However, within a year, Hitler began to break the agreement and attack the Catholic Church. Its schools were made to remove Christian symbols, such as the crucifix, from the classrooms. And later the schools were taken away from Church control. In 1937, the Catholic Youth was made illegal.

Many priests opposed these Nazi policies and as a consequence were arrested. At least 400 priests were put in a special block in Dachau concentration camp. The Pope, Pius XI, wanted to avoid conflict with the Nazis, but by 1937 he had lost patience. He showed his opposition to Hitler's policies in a famous statement known as 'With Burning Anxiety'.

Hitler's policies did not destroy the Catholic Church. In many respects, they had the opposite effect. Priests who were sent to concentration camps were seen as martyrs. Church leaders were often applauded by the people when they appeared in public. And Catholic churches were packed with worshippers every Sunday.

The Protestant Church

Protestants became divided in their attitude to the Nazis.

Reich Church

In 1933, those Protestant groups that supported the Nazis agreed to unite to form the 'Reich Church'. Their leader, Ludwig Müller, became the first *Reich* bishop in September 1933. The keenest members of the *Reich* Church called themselves 'German Christians', wore Nazi uniforms and gave the Nazi salute. Their motto was 'The swastika on our chests and the Cross in our hearts.'

Confessional Church

Many Protestant, pastors opposed Hitler and the Reich Church. They were led by Pastor Martin Niemöller, who set up the 'Confessional Church'. More than 6,000 pastors supported this Church. Niemöller and many other pastors were arrested by the Nazis and sent to concentration camps. Niemöller survived and he was released by the Allies in 1945. Nazi repression did not destroy Protestant opposition. Instead, once again, it created Protestant martyrs.

examzone

Build better answers

Why did the Nazi Party oppose the Catholic Church? Explain your answer.

You may use the following in your answer:
• Catholics' first allegiance
• Catholic schools

You must also include information of your own. (12 marks)

  Basic, Level 1

Answer makes generalised statements without support from detail OR gives detail on a limited aspect of the question, for example: *Catholic schools had a different curriculum.*

  Good, Level 2

Answer understands the focus of the question and uses detail about the stimulus material to support their answer, for example: The Catholic schools did not teach Nazi propaganda, so they were not producing 'good Nazi citizens'. For top marks, students must use information of their own, for example: *Catholic parents sent their children to Catholic youth groups, not to the Hitler youth.*

▲ **Excellent, Level 3**

Answer uses accurate detail from the stimulus material and own knowledge to analyse the question and evaluate the impact of the various reasons, for example considering how the Catholic Church not only did not fully support the Nazis, but had a belief system that meant that Catholics saw the Pope as the person they should ultimately obey, not Hitler.

63

Activities

1 List three differences between Nazism and Christianity.

2 Draw a spider diagram showing reasons why the Nazis were against the Catholic Church.

3 Why did many Catholics and Protestants oppose Nazi policies towards the Churches? You may use the following in your answer and any other information of your own.

   • Catholic Churches and youth movements
   • Pastor Niemöller
   • Christian beliefs.

4 'The Nazis were successful in controlling the Churches in Germany in the years after 1933.' Do you agree or disagree with this statement?

   • Explain the aims of Nazi policies
   • identify any successful policies
   • identify any failures
   • decide how successful overall the Nazis were in their policies towards the Churches, with your reasons.

Summary

● The Nazis set up a police state to force people to support their regime. The main instruments of the police state were the SS and the *Gestapo*.

● The Nazis also used censorship to control what people saw and heard.

● Goebbels made use of many propaganda methods, such as posters, the radio and film, to try to persuade people to support Nazi ideals.

● The Catholic and Protestant Churches were persecuted by the Nazis. Many priests and pastors resisted and were sent to concentration camps.

2.3 Opposition and resistance to the Nazi government

Learning outcomes

By the end of this topic, you should be able to:

- understand reasons for opposition to the Nazi government
- explain the activities of opposition groups
- describe the successes and failures of these opposition groups.

Activities

1 Write down three reasons why some people opposed the Nazis.

2 What similarities are there in what happened to those who opposed the Nazis?

Edelweiss: This flower was the symbol on the badges worn by members of the Edelweiss Pirates. It also means noble or white

Getting an overview

The Nazi police state made opposition very difficult. Nevertheless, there were certain groups that opposed the Nazi ideals.

The 'Edelweiss Pirates'

Some young people opposed Nazi ideas. One such group was the Edelweiss Pirates. They listened to forbidden 'Swing' music and wrote anti-Nazi graffiti on walls. By 1939 there were 2,000 members.

The White Rose Group

The White Rose Group was started by students at Munich University. The leaders were Professor Kurt Huber and two students, Hans and Sophie Scholl. They gave out leaflets during the Second World War encouraging Germans not to help the war effort. They were arrested in 1943 and executed.

Pastor Martin Niemöller

Niemöller disliked the new German 'Reich Church' and set up the Confessional Church. He criticised Nazi policies and was arrested and sent to a concentration camp (he survived and was still alive when it was liberated by the Allies in 1945).

Dietrich Bonhoeffer

Bonhoeffer was a Church leader who spoke out against Nazi ideas. During the Second World War he helped Jews escape to Switzerland. He was arrested by the *Gestapo* in 1943 and sent to a concentration camp. He was executed in April 1945.

Colonel Claus von Stauffenberg

In the 1930s von Stauffenberg was a supporter of the Nazis. However, during the Second World War he witnessed the suffering of the German army in Russia and plotted to kill Hitler. The assassination attempt in July 1944 failed and Stauffenberg was arrested and executed.

Church opposition

Many Christians in Germany opposed the
Nazis, including Pastor Martin Niemöller and
Dietrich Bonhoeffer.

Martin Niemöller

Niemöller was a U-boat commander during the
First World War. After the war, he studied theology
and in 1924 became a pastor in the German
Protestant Church. In 1933, he welcomed Nazism
believing that Hitler would restore the greatness of
Germany and reverse the Treaty of Versailles. Like
the Nazis, he opposed the communists.

However, his views changed when the Nazis set up
the *Reich Church*, which Niemöller believed was
much more about Nazism than Christianity. In
1934 he established the rival German Confessional
Church which made clear differences between the
two. Over the next three years, Niemöller frequently
spoke out in public against the Nazi regime.

Source A: From one of Niemöller's last sermons before
his arrest in 1937.

> 'We must use our powers to free ourselves from the
> oppressive hand of the authority like the Apostles
> of old did. We are not willing to remain silent by
> decision of man when God commands us to speak.'

Hitler, furious at Niemöller's outspoken attacks,
ordered his arrest in July 1937. Niemöller was put
on trial the following year and given seven months
in prison. On his release, he continued to openly
attack the Nazi regime and was re-arrested and then
imprisoned in Sachsenhausen concentration camp
as a 'personal prisoner of the *Führer*'. Niemöller
survived the next seven years and was still alive
when the concentration camp was liberated by the
Allies in 1945.

Dietrich Bonhoeffer

Bonhoeffer was a Church leader who, in 1934,
helped Niemöller found the Confessional Church.
He believed that Christianity could not accept Nazi
racist views and that churchmen had to be free
to preach against the Nazis. He openly spoke out
against the Nazis, especially the Nuremberg Laws
of 1935, and, in 1937, the *Gestapo* banned him
from preaching.

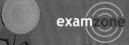

examzone

Build better answers

Why was there so little opposition to Hitler from
the Churches in Germany in the years 1934-1945?
Explain your answer.
You may use the following in your answer:
• the Concordat
• the Reich Church
You must also include information of your own.

(12 marks)

■ **Basic, Level 1**

Answer makes generalised statements without
support from detail OR gives detail on a limited
aspect of the question, for example: *the Catholics
reached an agreement with the Nazis.*

● **Good, Level 2**

Answer understands the focus of the question and
uses detail about the bullet points to support their
answer, for example: *there were Protestants that
were part of the Reich Church, the official Church
of the country.* Better answers also use information
of their own, for example that some of these
churches displayed the Nazi flag.

▲ **Excellent, Level 3**

Answer uses accurate detail from the bullet points
and own knowledge to analyse the question and
evaluate the impact of the various reasons they
consider.

In 1939, Bonhoeffer joined the *Abwehr*, the German
counter-intelligence service, within which a
secret group was working to overthrow Hitler.
He helped set up 'Operation 7', which assisted a
small number of Jews to escape to Switzerland. In
1943 he was arrested by the *Gestapo* for plotting
against Hitler. He served the next two years in
solitary confinement before being transferred to a
concentration camp. In April 1945, not long before
the camp was liberated, Bonhoeffer was sentenced
to death and executed by the SS.

Youth opposition

Why did some young Germans oppose the Nazis?

Not all young people accepted Nazi attempts to convert them to their ideas through education and youth movements. By the end of the 1930s a number of gangs emerged who opposed Nazi attempts to control all aspects of their life. These included the 'Travelling Dudes' from Essen and the 'Navajos' from Cologne. As the war developed, however, these gangs began to organise opposition to the war itself.

The Edelweiss Pirates

Many of these gangs eventually became part of a national resistance group known as the Edelweiss Pirates, named after the distinctive **edelweiss** flower they used as an emblem. Pirates wore check shirts and dark trousers. At weekends they would go on hikes, meet other groups and hope to beat up Hitler Youth patrols.

Source A: Part of an Edelweiss Pirate song.

> We march by banks of Ruhr and Rhine
> And smash the Hitler Youth in twain.
> Our song is freedom, love and life,
> We're the Pirates of the Edelweiss.

During the Second World War they gathered up propaganda leaflets dropped by Allied bombers and pushed them through people's doors. They also provided shelter to deserters from the armed forces. In 1944 the Pirates killed the head of the Cologne *Gestapo*. A group of them were caught soon afterwards and hanged.

Source B: The public hanging of a group of resistance fighters, some of whom were 'Edelweiss Pirates'.

The White Rose Group

This group was set up by Hans and Sophie Scholl and Professor Kurt Huber at Munich University in 1941. Hans Scholl was a medical student who had served as a medical orderly on the Russian Front and had seen, first hand, the atrocities that were carried out against the Jews, the Poles and other non-Aryans (see pages 94-103). They believed that if they publicised these atrocities, then many Germans would support them in opposing the Nazis. The White Rose was a symbol of their belief in justice. In one of their pamphlets they wrote: 'We will not be silent. We are your bad conscience. The White Rose will not leave you in peace.'

These leaflets had to be issued anonymously, by leaving them in public places, on doorsteps or in postboxes. However, on 18 February 1943, Hans and Sophie Scholl were seen giving out leaflets by a caretaker at Munich University, who was also a Nazi Party member. The caretaker informed the *Gestapo* and the Scholls were arrested, tortured and beheaded. Sophie Scholl had her leg broken during *Gestapo* interrogation and had to limp to the scaffold on crutches. They were described as 'despicable criminals' in local newspapers.

Activities

1 Working in pairs, make a copy of and complete the following table to show the similarities and differences between the Edelweiss Pirates and the White Rose Group.

	Similarities	Differences
Aims		
Methods		
End		

2 The Nazis described the White Rose Group as 'despicable criminals'. Why are they now seen as heroes?

Army opposition

The most serious opposition to Hitler came from within the army. The army leaders had reluctantly supported Hitler during the early years of the Second World War, when German armies had, for the most part, been successful. However, defeats, especially on the Eastern Front, brought opposition from within the army, led by General Ludwig Beck. He supported plans by Count von Stauffenberg to assassinate Hitler.

Von Stauffenberg had witnessed the defeats on the Russian front. In 1943, while serving in the North African desert, he was badly wounded, losing his left eye, right arm and two fingers of his left hand. He was especially appalled by the brutality of the SS. He devised 'Operation Valkyrie' which involved using a bomb in a briefcase to kill Hitler. On 20 July 1944, Stauffenberg took the briefcase to a military conference in East Prussia. He placed it under a table, 2 metres away from Hitler. The bomb went off but the heavy table saved Hitler's life. Hitler was cut and deafened but still very much alive.

Hitler took savage revenge on all those involved in the 'July' plot. The total number executed came to 5,746, including von Stauffenberg and Beck. The dead included 19 generals and 26 colonels.

Source A: A member of Hitler's staff shows the trousers worn by Hitler when the bomb exploded.

Source B: From a study of opposition to the Third *Reich* written by M. Housden in 1994.

'The most significant efforts at resistance came from the establishment sections of German society, that is to say the minor nobility, civil servants and, most notably, members of the officer corps… In the Third *Reich*, a person needed courage just to say 'hello' to someone in the street wearing a yellow star. For that reason we must be careful not to undervalue the achievements of anyone who did anything, no matter how small. Equally we must stand in awe at the self-sacrificed heroism of a person such as von Stauffenberg. But just as we value bravery, we need to maintain a sense of proportion… While many Germans remained at odds with the Third *Reich*, only a few exceptional souls, driven by a mixture of bravery and despair, dared express themselves openly. But then, how many of us, today, under similar circumstances, would be different?'

Activities

1 What can you learn from Source B about opposition to the Nazis?

2 Group task. Which groups provided the most effective opposition to the Nazis?
   - the youth groups
   - the religious leaders
   - the army.

3 'Opposition and resistance groups in Nazi Germany failed to achieve anything.' Discuss.

Summary

- The police state made opposition and resistance to the Nazi regime both difficult and dangerous.

- There were a number of young people who opposed the Nazi government, including the Edelweiss Pirates and the White Rose Group.

- Two key Church leaders also spoke out against the Nazis – Niemöller and Bonhoeffer. They were arrested and sent to concentration camps.

- Members of the army, led by General Beck and von Stauffenberg, attempted unsuccessfully to assassinate Hitler in July 1944.

Quick quiz

1 Place the following events in chronological order

a) The *Reichstag* Fire	
b) The Nazis win 107 seats in the *Reichstag*	
c) The Enabling Act	
d) Schleicher becomes Chancellor	
e) The Nazis win 196 seats in the *Reichstag*	
f) The Night of the Long Knives	
g) Hitler becomes Chancellor	
h) The Nazis win 230 seats in the *Reichstag*	
i) Trades Unions are banned	
j) Papen becomes Chancellor	
k) Germany becomes a one-party state	

2 The Nazis used a mixture of terror and persuasion to bring about support for the Nazi regime.

a) Make a copy of the following table.

Terror	Persuasion

b) Organise the following methods into categories, either terror or persuasion, and complete your copy of the table. Add more rows if you need to.

radio *Gestapo* **concentration camps**
***Reich* Church Concordat with the Pope**
SS Nuremberg rallies control of art
posters cinema cult of *Führer*
one-party state

3 Make a copy of the following account of opposition to the Nazis and use the words given below to complete the gaps:

It was very _____ to oppose the Nazi government. However, some groups and _____ were prepared to do this. One such group was the _____ _____ who were named after a flower. A second group, the _____ _____ _____ was set up during the Second World War. The leaders of both these groups were eventually captured and _____. A member of the army, Colonel _____ organised a plot to blow up Hitler. The bomb did go off but Hitler _____. Hitler was also opposed by Church leaders such as _____ _____. He was arrested for criticising the Nazi government and sent to a _____ camp.

individuals executed Edelweiss Pirates
dangerous von Stauffenberg pastor
concentration Martin Niemöller survived
White Rose Group

Plenary activities

Work in groups on this activity.

The following individuals and groups helped or hindered Hitler in his rise to power and establishment of a dictatorship of the Nazi Party.

1 Make a copy of the following table.

Helped	Hindered

2 Categorise the following groups and individuals under the headings 'Helped' or 'Hindered' giving a brief explanation for each. (You may need to place some in both columns.)

Hugenberg   communists   Hindenburg SA   Papen   big business   Schleicher Gestapo   Goebbels   Catholic Church Röhm   Protestant Church

Checklist

How well do you know and understand?

- ◗ The reasons why Hitler was invited to become Chancellor in January 1933.
- ◗ The methods Hitler used to remove opposition in the years 1933–1934.
- ◗ Hitler's role as *Führer*.
- ◗ The key features of the Nazi police state.
- ◗ Censorship and propaganda used by the Nazis.
- ◗ Nazi policies towards the Churches.
- ◗ Reasons for opposition to the Nazi government.
- ◗ The activities of opposition groups.
- ◗ The successes and failures of these opposition groups.

Student tip

Candidates often confuse the two command words 'Describe' and 'Explain'. If a question asks about an event:

- **Describe** means give precise details, generally in the correct sequence, of a key event.

- **Explain** is asking for developed causes or consequences of an event. For example, an explanation of the reasons for increased support for the Nazis in the years 1929–1932.

The social impact of the Nazi state to 1945

Introduction

The Nazis had very definite views about the society they wished to create and the roles of men and women within that society. Women were to return to their traditional role as mothers and wives while men were to run the country and fight in the armed forces. Moreover, Hitler was determined to create the 'Thousand Year *Reich*', an empire which would last a very long time. This would be dependent on the support of future generations. Consequently, much effort was made to control the thoughts and actions of the young and ensure they believed in and followed Nazi ideals.

The Nazis also made changes to the economy, with the emphasis on rearmament. In addition, through a variety of schemes (some more dubious than others), they more or less eliminated unemployment. There is still much debate about the quality of life under the Nazis. Were Germans better off? Many more had work, but they also had far less freedom.

Hitler had very distinct racial views and was determined to create an Aryan master race, i.e. a race of people from pure Germanic stock. This, in turn, meant the removal of any groups that threatened this master race, most especially the Jews. The Nazis systematically increased the persecution of the Jews after 1933 in an effort to force them out of Germany. The outbreak of the Second World War and the expansion of German territory greatly increased the number of Jews under Nazi control. And this, in turn, led to the 'Final Solution', the setting up of camps to exterminate European Jews.

Anti-semitic Nazi propaganda.

Advertising the Nazi lifestyle.

A sketch by a concentration camp survivor.

Aims and outcomes

By the end of this section, you should be able to understand, describe and explain...

- how the Nazis changed the roles of women and tried to control the lives of the young
- whether German people were better off under the Nazis
- Nazi policies towards the Jews and other minority groups in the years 1933–1945.

1933

Boycott of Jewish shops. Introduction of the Labour Front.

A poster showing members of the Hitler Youth.

FASCINATING FACT

The position of women changed dramatically under the Nazis. For example, look at the advertisement below for a wife, which appeared in a German newspaper in 1935: *Wanted – young, healthy, virgin of pure Aryan stock, undemanding, suited to heavy work and thrifty with flat heels, without earrings, if possible without money.*

Activities

1 Study the three small illustrations on the opposite page.

   a) Use one word to summarise each illustration.

   b) Which gives the best image of life in Nazi Germany?

2 The poster on this page was used as a propaganda poster. Devise a suitable propaganda caption.

1934	1935	1936	1937	1938	1939	1942	1945
chacht ade Minister of Economics.	*Reich* National Service Law. Nuremberg Laws.	First Hitler Youth Law.	Adolf Hitler Schools set up.	*Kristallnacht.*	Setting up of ghettos for Jews. Unemployment down to 300,000. 3 September: Start of Second World War.	Introduction of the 'Final Solution'.	7 May: End of Second World War in Europe.

3.1 Nazi policies towards women and the young

Learning outcomes

By the end of this topic, you should be able to:

● understand Nazi policies towards women

● explain Nazi policies towards the young

● describe the successes and failures of these policies.

Conscription: Compulsory military service

Eugenics: Study of improving the qualities of the human race

Labour exchanges: Job centres

Lebensraum: Living space

Activities

1 Study the diagram below. Identify two things you can learn about women and their roles in Nazi Germany.

2 Write down three changes that women experienced under the Nazis.

Getting an overview

Appearance

The 1920s saw new fashions for women including short hair, make-up and shorter skirts. Women began to smoke and drink in public. The Nazis believed in the traditional natural appearance with long hair, no make-up and long skirts. Women were discouraged from smoking and drinking.

Employment

There had been progress in women's employment opportunities in the 1920s, especially in the more professional careers in teaching and medicine. The Nazis reduced the number of women, especially married women, in employment. However, due to rearmament, more women were employed in industry after 1937.

Marriage

Hitler wanted to increase the birth rate and encouraged German women to marry and have as many children as possible. Married couples were given loans based on the number of children they had.

Nazi aims

The Nazis believed in the traditional domestic role of women, which was to marry, have children and look after the home. Policies were designed to reinforce this. The Nazis were determined to turn the young into loyal Nazis and also train boys and girls for their different roles in later life.

Education

The Nazis used education and youth movements to control the lives of girls (and boys). Schooling and Nazi youth movements were used to prepare the young for their future roles in society – the girls for their domestic role and the boys for work and the army.

Women in Weimar Germany

There had been a number of changes in the position of women in Germany in the 1920s. In fact, Germany was ahead of Britain in political and employment rights for women.

- In 1919 women over the age of 20 were given the vote. This encouraged greater female interest in politics. Indeed by 1933 nearly one-tenth of *Reichstag* members were female.
- Many young women enjoyed much greater social freedom. They went out without a chaperone (someone to escort them) and smoked and drank in public places.
- There were major changes in their appearance. They wore short skirts, make-up and had their hair cut short.
- There was rapid progress in female employment opportunities. Many women now took up careers in the professions, especially the civil service and teaching. Indeed, in some careers women earned the same pay as men.

Source A: An advert for perfume from the 1920s that features the 'modern woman'.

Nazi aims

Source B: From Gertrud Scholtz-Klink, Head of the Nazi Women's Organisation.

'Woman is entrusted in the life of the nation with the great task, the care of man, soul, body and mind. It is the mission of woman to look after the home. Her role in marriage is as a comrade and helper to her husband – this is the right of woman in the New Germany.'

The Nazis wanted to reverse the developments of the 1920s so that women would return to their traditional role as homemakers and childbearers. This was for several reasons:

- Hitler genuinely believed in this traditional role, which he believed raised women to a very important place in society
- removing women from the job market would reduce the problem of unemployment
- the Nazis were determined to increase the birth rate and strengthen the Third *Reich*
- women had a central role in producing the genetically pure Aryan race and the future Nazi warriors
- the Nazi slogan '*Kinder, Küche, Kirche*' ('Children, Cooking and Church') summed up the role of women in Germany.

Source C: From an article published in Germany in 1933.

'There is no room for women who are interested in politics in Nazi Germany. All that this movement has ever said and thought on the subject goes against politics and women. Woman is relegated to her role as a mother and a wife. The German revolution is an event made by, and supremely concerned with, the male.'

Activity

1 What can you learn from Source B about the role of women in Nazi Germany?

Women and employment

From 1933 women were encouraged to give up their jobs, get married and have large families. Women doctors, civil servants and teachers were forced to leave their jobs. **Labour exchanges** and employers were encouraged to give the first choice of jobs to men.

Girls were discouraged from going on to higher education, so that they would not have the qualifications for professional careers. Indeed, generous social security benefits were given to encourage women to stay at home.

Marriage and the family

In 1933 the Law for the Encouragement of Marriage was introduced. This provided loans to help young couples to marry, as long as the wife left her job. For each child, up to four children, couples were allowed to keep one-quarter of the loan. A number of other policies encouraged more births and laws against abortion were strictly enforced. Birth-control clinics were closed down and a massive propaganda campaign was launched to promote the importance of the mother and the family. The government also increased maternity benefits.

On Hitler's mother's birthday (12 August) medals were awarded to women with larger families:

- gold for eight or more
- silver for six children
- bronze for five children.

Additionally, a new national organisation, called the German Women's Enterprise, organised classes and radio talks on household topics and the skills of motherhood.

Women's appearance

The ideal Nazi woman was fair-haired, blue-eyed and sturdily built. She was expected to have broad hips for childbearing and to wear traditional clothes, not fashionable ones. She would not wear make-up, nor did she smoke or drink. Slimming was frowned upon because being slim was considered bad for childbearing.

Activities

2 Explain how the Nazis changed the role of women in the years after 1933.

Source D: A poster produced in 1935 by the Organisation to Aid Mothers and Children. It says 'Germany grows through strong mothers and healthy children.'

Source E: A sketch by a Nazi artist showing the ideal Nazi woman.

How successful were the Nazi policies regarding women in achieving their aims?

There were successes. In the first few years the number of married women in employment fell. Moreover, the number of marriages increased and there was a rise in the birth rate. The German Women's Enterprise Organisation had 6 million members. It organised 'Mother's Schools' to train women in household skills, as well as courses, lectures and radio programmes on household topics.

For many women these were good times. Those who had been hardest hit by the depression were much better off by 1935. Those who had been able to find employment found that their wages were rising faster than prices.

However, there were limitations and even failures. The rise in the birth rate may have been due to the economic recovery of the period rather than Nazi policies. Most couples continued to have families of two children.

Moreover, the number of women in employment actually increased from 4.85 million in 1933 to 7.14 million six years later. From 1936, there was a labour shortage and the Nazis needed more workers in heavy industry because of rearmament. In 1937, the Nazis changed the marriage loans scheme to allow married women who had been given a loan to take up employment. Many employers preferred women workers because they were cheaper. Women's wages remained only two-thirds of a man's.

Source F: From a history of Germany 1918–1945, written in 1997.

'In their efforts the Nazis enjoyed some success. The numbers of working women only rose from 4.8 million in 1932 to 5.9 million in 1937, but because more men than women were taking jobs, this was really a fall from 37% to 31% of the total work force. But women were really too useful to the German economy to remove them completely from the work force. As the Nazis geared Germany up for war, women provided cheap and reliable labour. The Nazis relaxed the restrictions of women working from 1938. The Nazis were caught in the contradictions of their position.'

Source G: From a history of Germany, written in 2001.

'In some areas, such as women's organisations and youth groups, the Nazis widened experiences for women. Social services improved. Opportunities to avoid the drudgeries of paid employment had advantages. Furthermore, several historians now stress the ineffectiveness of many Nazi restrictions. This is not to deny that for many women (though proportionately a small number) as well as men their experience of the regime was horrific.'

Source H: Women's employment in millions.

Married women working outside the home	Total (millions)
1933	4.2
1939	6.2*

*35% of married women aged 16–65.

Activities

3 According to Sources F and G, did the position of women in Nazi Germany improve?

4 'Nazi policies towards women were a failure.' To what extent do you agree with this view? Working in pairs, evaluate the following:

- the successes of the Nazi policies
- the limitations and failures.

Make a final assessment and give your reasons.

5 'Women in Nazi Germany were different, not inferior.' Discuss.

The Nazis and young people

Source A: Bernhard Rust, the Nazi Minister of Education.

> 'The whole purpose of education is to create Nazis.'

The Nazis were determined to turn the young into loyal Nazis. In addition they wanted to train boys and girls for their different roles in later life. The Nazis tried to achieve this aim by controlling education during the weekdays and youth movements in the evenings and weekends.

Activities

1 What can you learn from Source A about the Nazis and education?
2 Write down one difference and two similarities in the education and youth movements of girls and boys.

Nazi control of education

The Nazis used education as a method of indoctrinating the young with Nazi ideas, that is, teaching them to accept their views. This was achieved by controlling all aspects of education.

It became compulsory for teachers to join the Nazi Party and swear an oath of loyalty. Many teachers attended teachers' camps, which concentrated on how to indoctrinate the young and on physical training. Nearly all teachers joined the Nazi Teachers' Association.

The curriculum was carefully organised to put across key Nazi ideals:

- Lessons began and ended with the teachers and pupils saluting and saying 'Heil Hitler'.
- History was rewritten to glorify Germany's past and the rise of the Nazi Party. History books attacked the Treaty of Versailles and blamed Jews and communists for Germany's past problems.
- Physical education occupied 15 per cent of school time to ensure that girls were fit to be mothers and boys were prepared for military service. Pupils had to pass a physical examination or else they could be expelled from school.
- **Nazi Eugenics** was a new subject that taught pupils about selective breeding, more especially the creation of a master race. Pupils were taught that they were not to marry inferior racial types, such as Jews.
- Race studies was another new subject. This put forward Nazi ideas of race, in particular the superiority of the Aryan race and the inferiority of the sub-humans, the Jews. Pupils were taught how to measure their skulls and to classify racial types.
- In geography pupils were taught about lands that were once part of Germany and the need for more *Lebensraum* (that is, land to inhabit) for Germans.

Nazi textbooks

From 1935, all textbooks had to be centrally approved by the Nazis. New textbooks were produced reflecting Nazi ideals.

Nazi schools

Everyone in Germany had to go to school until the age of 14. After that, schooling was optional. The Nazis moved away from co-education to separate schools and curriculums for the two sexes.

- Boys took science, maths and military drilling. Schooling for boys concentrated on physical fitness and military fitness and skills to prepare them for the armed forces.
- Girls took needlework, music, language and homecrafts. Female education was designed to prepare girls for marriage and motherhood with the emphasis on domestic duties as well as physical fitness.

Source B: Extract from a Nazi history textbook about a First World War battle.

'A Russian soldier tried to get in his way, but Otto's bayonet slid gratingly between his ribs, so that he collapsed groaning. There it lay before him, simple and distinguished, his dream's desire, the Iron Cross.'

Source C: A German father describes a mathematics question in his son's textbook.

'When Klauss got back from school at five o'clock he bullied me into helping him with his homework. Here is a maths problem picked out at random: "A plane on take off carries 12 bombs, each weighing 10 kilos. The aircraft makes for Warsaw, the centre of international Jewry. It bombs the town. On take-off with all the bombs on board and a fuel tank containing 1,500 kilos of fuel the aircraft weighed 8 tonnes. When it returned from the crusade, there were still 230 kilos of fuel left. What is the weight of the aircraft when empty?"'

Source D: An illustration from a textbook shows a Jewish 'sex-fiend' passing out sweets to children.

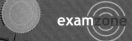
Build better answers

What can you learn from Source D about education in Nazi Germany?

(4 marks)

■ **Basic, Level 1**

Answer makes an inference but does not use the source to support it, for example: *the Nazis were against the Jews or they used propaganda.*

● **Good, Level 2**

Answer uses the source to support the inference, for example: *the source shows that propaganda was used in education. There was propaganda against the Jews in school textbooks, where the Jew is shown as an ugly 'sex-fiend'. The Jewish man is shown as a danger to children to encourage hatred of Jews.*

Teachers were controlled by the Nazi Party, who issued regulations concerning the curriculum, while teachers themselves were expected to join the Nazi Party. The Nazis also established a network of schools outside the state system, which were to prepare future leaders. For example, the National Political Educational Institutes were for students aged between 10 and 18. These were run by the SS and trained future leaders of the military and the administration. In addition, there were Adolf Hitler Schools to provide future Party leaders. The best students from these schools went on to the 'Order Castles' for the future elite leaders of the Third *Reich*. Here there was intense political and physical training.

Source E: A timetable for a girls' school.

A typical timetable from a girls' school. German children went to school six days a week, including Saturdays.

8.00 German (every day)
8.50 Geography, history or singing
9.40 Race study or ideology (3 days each)
10.25 Break
11.00 Domestic science with maths (every day)
12.10 Eugenics or health biology (3 days each)

Most afternoons would be spent in sport.

(Eugenics is the study of improving the human race in order to produce perfect Aryan babies.)

Source F: From *A Boy in Your Situation,* written in 1988.

The new school was not a happy place. Karl's new teacher introduced himself. He wore a button with a *swastika* on it in his lapel buttonhole.

'I must now make up the register. Hartland, the banker? Are you Jewish?'

'Yes'.

'What a pity. I had hoped for a completely Aryan class.'

Source G: Extracts from the history curriculum recommended by the *Nationalist Socialist Educator.*

Weeks	Subject	Relations to Jews
1–4	Pre-war Germany The class war Profits, strikes	The Jew at large!
5–8	From agrarian to industrial state Colonies	The peasant in the claws of the Jews
9–12	Conspiracy against Germany	The Jew reigns War plots
13–16	German struggle German want Blockade! Starvation!	The Jew becomes prosperous! Profit from German want
17–20	The stab in the back Collapse	Jews as leaders of the November insurrection
21–24	Germany's Golgotha Erzberger's crimes! Versailles	Jews enter Germany from the east. Judah's triumph

Activities

3 Study Sources B–G on pages 77–78. Make a copy of the following table, explaining what Nazi ideas are being put across in each source.

Source	Nazi ideas

4 In what ways was the curriculum designed to indoctrinate young people?

5 Describe the role of education in controlling the young in Nazi Germany.

Nazi Youth movements

The Nazis also wanted to control the young in their evening, weekend and holiday leisure time. They quickly closed down all youth movements belonging to other political parties as well as those of the Churches.

Source A: Hitler speaking in 1933.

> 'My program for educating youth is hard. Weakness must be hammered away. In my castles of the Teutonic Order a youth will grow up before which the world will tremble. I want a brutal, domineering, fearless, cruel youth. Youth must be all that. It must bear pain. There must be nothing weak and gentle about it. The free, splendid beast of prey must once again flash from its eyes… That is how I will eradicate thousands of years of human domestication… That is how I will create the New Order.'

Under Nazi rule four separate organisations were developed that recruited girls and boys from the age of 10 to 18 under the control of Baldur von Shirach, Youth Leader of the *Reich*.

Deutsches Jungvolk Young German folk Boys aged 10–14	*Jung Mädel* Young Girls Girls aged 10–14	*Hitler Jugend* Hitler Youth Boys aged 14–18	*Bund Deutscher Mädel* League of German Maidens Girls aged 14–18

Source B: A recruiting poster for the League of German Maidens.

Hitler Youth activities were based on competition, physical fitness and military training. Youth leaders organised hundreds of sporting contests and other activities, such as hiking. Boys were prepared for the army with frequent drilling, practice in shooting, map-reading and signalling. There were also annual military style camps that encouraged teamwork and comradeship. And lessons were given to reinforce Aryan superiority, the importance of the state and the *Führer*, and other Nazi ideals.

Source C: Members of the Hitler Youth camping.

Girls were kept totally separate from boys. As well as physical fitness and indoctrination in Nazi ideals, the main emphasis was on preparing them for motherhood by teaching domestic skills. The girls were taught how to make beds and cook.

The Hitler Youth Law of 1936 made it virtually impossible for any young person to avoid joining one of the Hitler Youth organisations. Three years later, the Second Hitler Youth Law made membership of the Hitler Youth compulsory. Members of the Hitler Youth had to swear an oath of loyalty to the *Führer*.

How successful was the Hitler Youth in achieving its aims?

Membership of the Hitler Youth expanded from 5.4 million in 1936 to 8 million in 1939. Many young people enjoyed the exciting and interesting activities, such as camping and hiking. Some even enjoyed the military aspects of the youth movements, especially the uniforms and discipline. For others it gave a great sense of comradeship and of belonging to something that seemed powerful.

Many parents approved of the Hitler Youth. They liked their children being part of a group. Most of the camps and activities were free. Parents also approved of the charity work Hitler Youth groups were involved in. They worked hard for the Winter Help organisation, which provided food, fuel and other supplies to the poor in winter. They also collected donations for different 'drives' that the local areas organised.

Source D: Henrik Metelmann describes what it was like being a member of the Hitler Youth in the 1930s.

'It was a great feeling. You felt you belonged to a great nation again. Germany was in safe hands and I was going to help to build a strong Germany. But my father of course felt differently about it. He warned "Now Henrik, don't say to them what I am saying to you." I always argued with my father as I was very much in favour of the Hitler regime which was against his background as a working man.'

Source E: A. Klonne, writing in 1982, remembers the Hitler Youth.

'What I liked about the Hitler Youth was the comradeship. I was full of enthusiasm. What boy isn't fired by high ideals such as comradeship, loyalty, honour. The trips off into the countryside. I was pleased that sport had its place. Later when I became a leader the negative aspects became obvious. I found the compulsion and the requirement of absolute obedience unpleasant. It was preferred that people should not have a will of their own. The Hitler Youth was interfering everywhere in people's lives. In our troop the activities consisted almost entirely of boring military drill.'

However, at least three million young people had not joined the Hitler Youth by the end of 1938. They could not be forced to join, although they were heavily 'encouraged'. Some who joined it were not enthusiastic members. Not all adults were enthusiastic either. Some teachers and parents were concerned about the effects of so much propaganda and about the effects on family life of Hitler Youth membership, although few voiced their objections too openly, for fear of arrest. Members of Hitler Youth groups were encouraged to see Hitler as their father and the group as their family. It encouraged them to report any instances of 'disloyalty' by other family members to the *Gestapo*. They were encouraged to challenge parental authority and spend very little time at home.

Activities

1 Why might Sources C and D have attracted young Germans to join the Hitler Youth?

2 To what extent were the experiences of girls and boys of the Hitler Youth similar, and to what extent were they different?

Source F: From *Inside Hitler's Germany*, by B. Sax and D. Kuntz, written in 1992.

'What National Socialist training produced, however, were duller and stupider, though healthier, individuals. By the late 1930s, the authorities became increasingly aware of the fact that while students, no longer able to think for themselves, would therefore not resist the regime, they were incapable of either providing political leadership in the future or contributing the intellectual and technical skills necessary for running a modern industrial society.'

Activities

3 What can you learn from Source F about the effects of Nazi control of the young?

4 Working in groups, examine the evidence for and against the success of the Nazis' policies in education and youth movements in controlling the young.

5 How far do you agree that Nazi policies were successful in controlling the young?

 exam zone
Build better answers

Describe the ways in which the Nazi Party used youth groups in the years 1933-1939. (9 marks)

■ **Basic, Level 1**
Answer makes generalised statements without support from detail OR gives detail on a limited aspect of the question.

● **Good, Level 2**
Answer gives some examples, with some accurate supporting detail. For example: *that they used them to expose children more to Nazi ideas in their time out of school. They used them to make the children fit, because the Nazis thought that was important.*

▲ **Excellent, Level 3**
Answer understands the focus of the question and considers Nazi motivation as well as just the activities of the youth groups. For example: *that the Nazis used youth groups to turn young children into good Nazis, teaching them Nazi propaganda and loyalty to Hitler. They also made them fit for motherhood or the army, depending on if they were girls or boys.*

81

1933
All other youth associations banned

1935
All new textbooks for schools had to be approved

1936
The Hitler Youth Law gave the Hitler Youth the same status as home and school

1937
Adolf Hitler Schools set up

1938
Membership of Hitler Youth reached 7 million

1939
The Second Hitler Youth Law made membership of the Hitler Youth compulsory

The war years

Women

The Nazis struggled with their attitudes to women and work during the war years. Many important Nazis, including Hitler, thought that, even during the war, only unmarried working class women should work. Even then they only wanted them to do 'suitable' work, not heavy manual labour. This included munitions work – women were doing this from 1936, while Germany re-armed. So the number of working women rose from 1936.

The war took millions of men into the armed forces. Someone had to do the jobs they left and cope with increased production in munitions factories. The Labour Ministry and the Armaments Ministry both urged the government to recruit more women. So the government began a propaganda drive, which had some effect. Then, as Germany captured more and more land to the east, well over a million women from areas such as Poland were forced to work in Germany. After this, the government began to call up childless married women and some others. It wasn't until 1943 that German women were widely conscripted.

The DFW (the women's section of the DAF) and the NSF (the National Socialist Women's Organisation) were set up in the early 1930s. They had focused on the Nazi ideal of women as mothers. During the war, their focus changed.

- The NSF focused on the 'home battlefront'. They taught women how to manage to feed their families on rations. They trained them to help in hospitals and fight fires. They also organised the evacuation of children and the distribution of ration coupons.
- The DFW organised women's work in munitions factories and also allocated women to the most vital jobs in other industries and elsewhere. These organisations only dealt with German women workers and worked hard to make sure they had reasonable working conditions. The Ministry of Labour dealt with forced labour of women from captured areas, such as Poland. Their working and living conditions were very basic.

Source A: From a letter written by a serving soldier to the labour office in his home town, Görlitz, in 1941.

> My wife has written that she has received from you a demand that she report for work. Just to make matters quite clear, I have forbidden my wife to go out to work as our baby is not yet two years old and, as far as I know, women who have small children shouldn't go to work, at least that's how our *Führer* wants it to be.

Source B: German women training as fire-fighters.

Young people

Even before the war, the Hitler Youth (HJ, for boys) and the League of German Maidens (BDM) had made charity collections, collected scrap metal and worked on farms. During the war, even very young people were expected to help the war effort.

The Home Front

From 1940, the HJ worked with the NSF on the children's evacuation programme, which sent mothers and their young children to foster homes in the countryside and older children to 'evacuation camps'. The older members of the BDM worked in these camps, cooking, cleaning and organising classes. They also worked with the Red Cross and in hospitals. They trained as fire fighters. They ran crèches for the children of mothers who were working and took over teaching in primary schools where there were not enough teachers. Younger members knitted gloves and socks for the troops and collected both money and recycling.

In 1940 a Nazi journal admitted the harvest could not have been collected without the youth groups. From April 1942, boys and girls were sent to work on farms all over Germany. About 600,000 boys and 1,400,000 girls worked on farms that year.

The HJ were trained for active and dangerous war work. When the heavy bombing of German cities began in 1942, the HJ fire services went into action, sometimes even while the bombs were still falling. Other HJ units cleared the bomb damage after the bombs had fallen and the fires were out. They searched for the dead and wounded and also for unexploded bombs.

From 1942, older members of the HJ were given military training in one of 142 special camps run by the army or the SS. By 1944, boys of 17 were being conscripted into the army with boys as young as 16 as volunteers. By 1945, boys as young as 13 were fighting. Younger Hitler Youth members manned anti-aircraft guns in towns, dug anti-tank ditches and carried messages at the front.

Rebels

Not all young people were members of Nazi youth groups but, as the war progressed, the Nazis came down even harder on young people who did not conform, even if they did not actively oppose the Nazis in the way that groups such as the Edelweiss Pirates (see page 66) did. The war meant that simply not belonging was opposition.

Summary

- The Nazis encouraged women not to work, but to be mothers and housewives.
- After 1936, they began to encourage single, working-class women to work in industry.
- During the war, they reluctantly encouraged more women to work, but they also used women workers from lands captured by Germany as forced labour.
- The Nazis tried to control the young by controlling the school curriculum and encouraging them to join Nazi youth groups.
- By the end of the 1930s, most young people were members of a Nazi youth group, even if unwillingly. Some children rebelled and refused to join.
- Nazi youth groups did valuable work during the war, on farms, in cities and even in the military services.

Activities

1 What can you learn from Source A about the problems faced by the government in trying to get women to work during the war?

2 Study Source B. Why might the government encourage women to train for such a dangerous occupation as fire-fighting?

3 Explain how the role of women changed during the years 1939-1945.

4 In pairs, discuss the work done by the HJ and the BDM during the war. Think about:
- the differences
- the similarities.

3.2 Economic changes

Learning outcomes

By the end of this topic you should be able to:

- understand Nazi attempts to reduce unemployment
- explain Nazi economic policies
- describe the standard of living enjoyed by the German people under the Nazis.

Autarky: Self-sufficiency

Autobahns: German motorways

Invisible unemployed: Unemployed not counted in official figures

Real wages: Wages adjusted to allow for inflation

Rearmament: Building up armed forces and weapons

Getting an overview

The Nazis were determined to reduce unemployment and build up the German armaments industry in readiness for a future war.

1933 Job creation schemes, especially the building of *autobahns*.

1934 Many women were forced to give up their jobs.

1935 National Labour Service was compulsory for all men between the age of 18 and 25. They spent six months working on public works schemes such as road building. Conscription was introduced for the German armed forces.

1936 Many Jews had been forced from their jobs.

1937 Rearmament led to the expansion of heavy industries such as iron and steel, coal, engineering, shipbuilding and the manufacture of tanks and military aircraft, and created jobs.

1938 Over one third of German spending was on rearmament which created more and more jobs.

1939 The German army had grown from 100,000 in 1933 to 1,400,000.

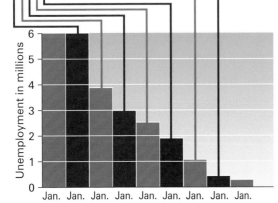

Better off	Worse off
In some ways Germans were better off under Hitler:	In other ways Germans were worse off under Hitler:
• most German men were in work • the 'Strength through Joy' organisation provided better leisure activities and holidays for workers • the 'Beauty Through Work' department improved working conditions, e.g. canteens and sports facilities • average weekly wages rose from 86 *marks* in 1932 to 109 *marks* in 1939 • the Volkswagen Scheme of 1938 gave workers the chance to buy cheap cars.	• Trades Unions were abolished and workers had few rights • few workers could afford the more expensive activities and holidays provided by 'Strength through Joy' • most German men did not enjoy National Labour Service, which was poorly paid • the cost of living went up in the 1930s – this cancelled out the rise in wages • average hours of work went up from 43 hours per week in 1933 to 47 in 1939 • the Volkswagen scheme turned out to be a swindle.

Activities

1 Identify three ways in which the Nazis reduced unemployment.
2 Give two examples of people being better off and two examples of people being worse off.

Nazi economic policies

German economic policy was dominated by two men and their plans:

- Dr Hjalmar Schacht: the New Plan (1933–1937); and
- Hermann Göring: the Four Year Plan (1936–1940).

Schacht and the New Plan

Dr Hjalmar Schacht was made President of the *Reichsbank* in 1933 and, the following year, Minister of Economics. His aims were to:

- reduce unemployment
- make Germany self-sufficient so it could survive future wars even if it was blockaded: this policy was known as **autarky**.

To achieve these he introduced the 'New Plan'. This plan was successful because it coincided with a revival in the world economy. Schacht succeeded in limiting German imports. He also made trade agreements with individual countries, by which they supplied Germany with essential raw materials in return for German goods. By 1935, Germany had a small trade surplus and production had increased by 50 per cent since 1933.

Schacht, however, resigned from his job in 1937 because he was against Hitler's plans to rearm quickly, arguing that the economy was not strong enough.

Göring and the Four Year Plan

From 1936, Germany's economic policy was increasingly controlled by Hermann Göring, a leading Nazi, who had little knowledge of the economy. His Four Year Plan dealt with preparing Germany for war within four years. The whole economy was geared towards **rearmament** and to making Germany self-sufficient in essential war materials, such as rubber, oil and steel.

The government poured millions of marks into the Four Year Plan. Business was persuaded to produce synthetic raw materials such as rubber, fuel and textiles. Textiles were made from pulped wood, rubber from coal, coffee from acorns and petrol from coal.

Activities

1 What is the message of Source A?
2 Which plan, the New Plan or the Four Year Plan, was more successful in achieving its aims? Explain your answer.

Source A: A poster encouraging German workers to help in the struggle for autarky. It says 'Help Hitler build. Buy German goods'.

However, these were not very successful and, in 1939, Germany was still dependent on foreign imports for its raw materials and oil.

New industrial plants, such as the Hermann Göring Works, which was a huge mining and metal works, were set up. Many of these used forced labour from the concentration camps. Arms production was given priority over consumer goods and agriculture. However, this led to food shortages and, in 1939, butter was still being rationed in Germany.

In fact the only way Germany could become fully self-sufficient was through foreign invasion and conquest. Some historians believe that the Four Year Plan was in crisis by 1939 and this forced Hitler to invade Poland.

How did the Nazis reduce unemployment?

When he became Chancellor in 1933, Hitler was determined to reduce unemployment and carry out the promises he had made in the years 1929–1932. In 1933, unemployment stood at 6 million and had fallen to less than half a million six years later. His policies seemed to have been more successful than those carried out by Britain, where unemployment fell from 3 million in 1933 to just under half that number in 1939. Germany's success was the result of several policies.

Job creation schemes

These were not new. The Weimar Republic had introduced a number of public works programmes in the years 1929–1933. Hitler, also, sought to create jobs through government spending on construction. In 1933, 18.4 billion *marks* was spent on these schemes, rising to 37.1 billion by 1938.

Germany built a network of motorways, known as *autobahns*, covering 7,000 km. This not only provided jobs, but also improved the efficiency of German industry by increasing the speed at which goods could cross the country, as well as enabling the swift transport of German troops. In addition, huge public buildings were constructed, for example, the stadium in Berlin for the 1936 Olympics.

The Nazis also subsidised private firms, especially in the construction industry, to stimulate the economy and provide more jobs. They invested money in the car industry, producing the Volkswagen or 'People's Car'. The German car industry as a whole expanded, which created jobs and reduced foreign car imports.

Source A: A poster promoting the *Deutsche Arbeitsfront* (DAF) or German Labour Front (see page 89). It says 'We Remain Comrades'.

National Labour Service

The National Labour Service was also not new. It had been started by the Weimar Republic and was continued by the Nazis. It was known as the *Reichsarbeitsdienst* or RAD and, in July 1935, it was made compulsory for all men aged between 18 and 25, who had to serve six months. This provided men to build the *autobahns*, as well as labour for other projects: for example, draining marshes to be used for farmland, tree planting, and building coastal walls to protect coastal areas from flooding.

The RAD removed thousands from the national unemployment figures. However, it was not popular. The workers were paid very low wages, and had to put up with uncomfortable tented camps, long hours of work and boring jobs.

Source B: A German remembers Labour Service.

'We work outdoors in all kinds of weather, shoveling dirt for very low pay. I'm trained as a printer. In the summer of 1933 I lost my job. I collected the dole until the spring of 1934. That was a lot better than what I am doing now. At least I was at home, with my family and could pick up odd jobs and work in the garden. Now I only get 10 days holiday a year.'

Invisible unemployment

The official government figures did not include a number of groups who lost their jobs or those in labour service without proper jobs. These people became the **invisible unemployed**.

Activities

1 Identify two things you can learn from Source A on the opposite page about the aims of the Labour Service.

2 Working in pairs, produce a mind map showing the main reasons why unemployment fell in Germany in the years 1933–1939.

- Prioritise the reasons within your mind map, beginning with the most important directly above the central box (at 12 o'clock) and then work your way round clockwise to finish with the least important.
- Explain your most important and least important reasons.
- Draw lines showing links between these reasons. Explain the links.

3 'Nazi policies hid, rather than reduced, the numbers out of work.' Discuss.

Jews	Women	Unmarried men	Opponents
From 1933, more and more Jews were forced out of their jobs, especially in the professions, such as lawyers and doctors.	Many women were dismissed from their jobs, especially in professional jobs. Others were tempted by state marriage loans to give up their jobs and marry.	Unmarried men under the age of 25 were forced to serve six months in National Labour Service.	In the early years of the Nazi government many opponents of Nazism, especially communists, were arrested and sent to concentration camps.

Rearmament

Rearmament became especially important in the years after 1936. The Four Year Plan changed the whole emphasis of the economy to preparing for a future war. The drive for rearmament created more jobs as more money was spent on manufacturing weapons. Billions were spent producing tanks, ships and aircraft. Heavy industry especially benefited.

In the years 1933–1939, production of coal and chemicals doubled, oil and iron and steel trebled, and iron ore extraction increased five-fold.

In addition, the expansion of the armed forces provided more jobs. When Hitler came to power the army was limited to just 100,000 men. By 1938, the figure had risen to 900,000.

The standard of living of German workers

There is much debate about the effects of Nazi policies on German workers. Were they better off or worse off under the Nazis?

Source A: A poster advertising the Volkswagen.

Source B: The memories of a farm worker from the 1930s.

'Thousands of people came from all over Germany to the Harvest Festival celebrations. We all felt the same happiness and joy. Harvest festival was the thank you for us farmers having a future again. I believe no statesman has ever been as well loved as Adolf Hitler was at that time. Those were happy times.'

Source C: Annual food consumption of German workers.

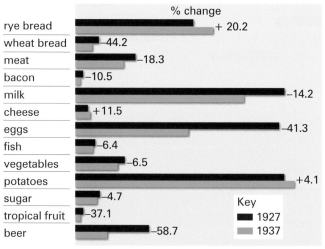

% change
- rye bread: +20.2
- wheat bread: −44.2
- meat: −18.3
- bacon: −10.5
- milk: −14.2
- cheese: +11.5
- eggs: −41.3
- fish: −6.4
- vegetables: −6.5
- potatoes: +4.1
- sugar: −4.7
- tropical fruit: −37.1
- beer: −58.7

Key
- 1927
- 1937

Activities

1 Make a copy of the following table.

Source	Workers benefited	Source	Workers did not benefit

Which of the three Sources on this page suggest workers benefited under the Nazis? Write these in your table with a brief explanation for each choice.

Which Sources suggest workers did not benefit? Write these in your table with a brief explanation for each choice.

2 Use the table to decide which statement you most agree with.
- German workers were better off under the Nazis.
- German workers were worse off under the Nazis.
- In some ways German workers were worse off under the Nazis.

Pay and hours of work

Under the Nazis, local and national pay rates were scrapped. Instead, wages were paid according to how much work you did. This method was fine for the young and healthy, but not for those who were older and could not produce as much.

From 1936 to 1939 wages actually increased, but this was due to a longer working day rather than an increase in hourly wage rates. Average working hours in industry actually increased from 42.9 hrs per week in 1933 to 47 hrs per week six years later. In addition, the cost of living increased during the early 1930s, which meant that **real wages** (what workers could buy) barely changed. All basic groceries cost more in 1939 than in 1933. There were also food shortages, because the government reduced agricultural production in order to keep up prices.

Source D: Real wages in Germany.

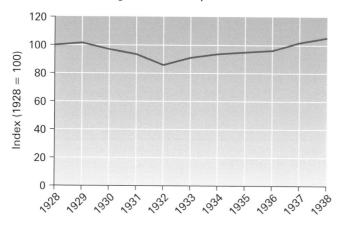

The Labour Front

The Nazis abolished Trade Unions and the worker's rights to negotiate for pay and hours of work. Trade Unions were considered a threat because they could organise strikes, which would threaten production. Moreover, the Unions were closely associated with the hated communists.

The Nazis wanted people to return to the idea of everyone working together. Trade Unions were replaced with the *Deutsche Arbeitsfront* (DAF) or German Labour Front led by Dr Robert Ley.

Membership of DAF was virtually compulsory for workers. It was different from a Union because it took on the full responsibility for the workplace and was determined to boost productivity.

At times, the DAF took the side of the employers and on other occasions it supported the workers. Above all, DAF tried to encourage workers to be motivated by a common spirit rather than wages and profit.

German Labour Front committees contained representatives of both employers and workers. These committees could only *recommend* higher wages or better working conditions. At first, the members of the committee would be elected. However, when it was found that opponents of the Nazi regime were elected in some cases, the Nazis abandoned elections in 1935. DAF ran two schemes to improve the working conditions and lifestyle of the workforce, *Schonheit der Arbeit* (SdA) meaning 'Beauty of Labour' and *Kraft durch Freude* (KdF) or 'Strength through Joy'.

Strength through Joy

The Strength through Joy scheme was set up to provide workers with activities when they were not working. It was hoped that this would result in happy workers who would be motivated to work harder. Those who worked hardest could be rewarded with a cruise on a KdF ship. In fact few managed this; for the majority the reward was cheap visits to concerts and the theatre.

Source E: Official Nazi figures showing activities provided by Strength through Joy in the Berlin area, 1933–1939.

Type of event	Number of events	Number of people involved
Theatre performances	21,146	11,507,432
Concerts	989	705,623
Hikes	5,896	126,292
Sports events	388	1,432,596
Cultural events	20,527	10,518,282
Holidays and cruises	1,196	702,491
Museum tours	61,503	2,567,596
Exhibitions	93	2,435,975
Weekend trips	3,499	1,007,242
Courses/lectures at the German Adult Education Office	19,060	1,009,922

Beauty of Labour

Known as the SdA, Beauty of Labour was another branch of the German Labour Front. Its main task was to improve working conditions, such as, for example, reducing the noise levels of machines. It also organised the building of canteens, swimming pools and sports facilities as well as better heating. Nevertheless, workers were expected to make these improvements in their spare time. This made the scheme less popular with many workers.

The Volkswagen

The scheme to build the Volkswagen was another function of the KdF. Hitler was keen to expand car ownership and encouraged the development of a new car, the Volkswagen, which means 'people's car'. It was to be cheap enough for workers to afford. A scheme was introduced in which workers paid 5 *marks* a week towards the cost of buying the car. However, by the time war broke out, not a single car had been bought and none of the money was refunded even though the cars were never made.

In 1939 production of the Volkswagen was switched to the needs of the military.

Source F: Hitler introducing the Volkswagen, 1938.

Activities

3 The Nazis almost certainly used Source F for propaganda purposes. Devise a suitable Nazi propaganda caption for the image.

4 Explain the importance of the KdF in Nazi Germany in the years after 1934.

5 Working in pairs, prepare a debate: 'Workers were better off under the Nazis.'

  • One of you should prepare the evidence in favour of this proposal.

  • The other should prepare the evidence against.

How well off were other groups under the Nazis?

Farming communities

The Nazis had gained strong support from farmers in the years after 1927. They flattered them with propaganda slogans, such as 'Blood and Soil'. Some farm debts were written off, and all farmers benefited from a rise in food prices. Farmers however suffered from a shortage of labour because workers left for better jobs in the towns.

Small business

The Nazis had also received much support from those in the small business sector, such as shopkeepers and craftsmen. The Nazis had promised to curb the influence of the large department stores and passed laws that banned the growth of the existing stores.

Big business

Big business really benefited from Nazi rule. There was no longer the worry about troublesome Trade Unions and the possibility of strikes. Rearmament resulted in growth and larger profits. Companies such as IG Farben gained huge government contracts to make explosives and even artificial oil from coal. The average salary of managers increased by nearly 70 per cent in the years 1934 to 1938. However, some industrialists did resent Nazi control of wages, profits, imports and raw materials.

What effects did the war have?

The war boosted the economy as war production took off. This reduced unemployment, as did **conscription** into the military. However, the war wasn't good for the economy in every way. It disrupted farming and trade, so food and fuel shortages became acute. Allied bombing disrupted transportation and services such as gas and electricity. It also damaged factories. The war created significant hardships for the civilian population.

Source A: M. Collier and P. Pedley, *Germany 1918–45*, published in 2001.

> 'Most workers enjoyed real wage rises after 1933 and skilled workers prospered with a return to full employment by 1936. At the same time the working week increased from an average of 40 hours in 1933 to 60 hours in 1944. Industrial accidents and industrial related illnesses rose by 150 per cent between 1933 and 1939. In addition, there was some working class unrest. There were strikes at Russelheim and Berlin in 1936 and a Party report from Nuremberg found open insubordination, sabotage, go-slows and absenteeism.'

Source B: W. Simpson, *Hitler and Germany*, published in 1991.

> 'The success or failure of Hitler's economic policies has been the subject of much debate. Unemployment was certainly cured, though whether this was due to a natural upturn in the world economy, work-creation schemes or rearmament is open to question. Heavy industry, iron and steel and chemicals showed a massive growth. The German Labour Front, through its promotion of organizations like "Strength through Joy" and "The Beauty of Labour", may have improved working conditions. But real wages barely rose between 1933 and 1939. Rearmament did not provide the resources for a large-scale war.'

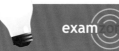
examzone **Top tip!**

You will improve your writing by supporting your exam answers with examples, which should be as detailed as possible. For this topic, this means being able to give some examples of Nazi economic policies, the various organisations set up to manage workers and the economic measures and other hardships that the war brought to German civilians.

Activities

1 Make a copy of and complete the following table, using Sources A and B.

Successes of Nazi policies	Shortcomings of Nazi policies

2 How successful were Nazi economic policies? You will need to consider the achievements and shortcomings of:
   - the policies of Schacht and Göring
   - measures to reduce unemployment
   - the standard of living.

3 'The Nazis sacrificed living standards in order to prepare for war.' Discuss.

91

1933
6 million out of work
Trade Unions banned
Introduction of the Labour Front

1934
Schacht made Minister of Economics

1935
Reich National Service Law

1936
Beginning of Göring's Four Year Plan

1938
Beginning of the Volkswagen scheme

1939
300,000 out of work
Start of War

1945
End of War

The Home Front

Germany had been preparing for war for some time before war broke out. Most people were not keen to go to war, but many trusted Hitler to do what was right for them and Germany. They also believed the propaganda that Germany would win the war quickly.

Food rationing

As soon as war broke out, pre-prepared food ration cards were distributed and rationing came into force. Bread, potatoes, butter, milk, cheese, eggs, sugar and cereals (e.g. oats or beans) were all rationed. Different workers were allowed different amounts of food, depending on whether they worked long hours or were doing 'heavy' work. Some workers (for example, those in munitions factories) were fed in a canteen in exchange for ration coupons. The rationing system was complicated but seemed fair to people.

However, by the start of 1942, there were shortages of many foods. Rationing now included fruit and vegetables. Food prices were government-controlled, but a black market grew up that ignored both rationing and price controls. People felt that the rich and powerful were much better fed than everyone else. The entry of the USA into the war, in December 1941, had damaged morale. Most people no longer believed government propaganda about Germany being bound to win the war.

Other supplies

Clothing was rationed. Other goods, such as shoes and soap, could only be bought with permits. Toilet paper ran out and making it was considered 'unnecessary', when people could use newspaper as a substitute. People were told to restrict the number of baths they took and how much fuel they used. From 1942, after losses in Russia, the Nazis announced a policy of 'total war'. No 'unnecessary' shops (e.g. sweet shops) could open. Sporting events and other entertainments were suspended and no more magazines were printed. People needed permits to buy furniture. From 1943, the effects of Allied bombing meant that household goods, such as pots, pans and crockery, were rationed. Again, a black market sprang up for all these things. Again, there were severe shortages, so that even people with ration coupons or permits could not buy what they needed.

Bombing raids

From March 1942, the Allies responded to the Nazi targeting of civilians in the Blitz with bombing raids of their own. The worst raids were against Hamburg in July 1943 and Dresden in February 1945. In each raid about 35-40,000 people were killed. Smaller raids on many cities killed fewer people but disrupted gas, electricity, water, road and rail services. Over 300,000 German civilians were killed and 750,000 injured in all these raids.

The government did their best to help the people who lost everything in the raids. They were told to register with the local authorities for replacement ration books and licences and for compensation for the loss of homes and property. There had been a housing shortage before the war. About two million homes were destroyed by bombing. By June 1943, the government had to take the unpopular step of re-housing the homeless in empty or 'underused' homes and offices.

Source A: A family rescued from the rubble after bombing in Mannheim in 1944.

Lawlessness

By 1945, wartime hardships had led to outbreaks of lawlessness and looting in parts of the country, which were almost impossible to control. People who ran the black market operations in these places had more real power than the government.

The situation was different in different parts of the country and for different groups of people. People did quite well if:

- they lived in farming communities where they could grow their own food, well away from places targeted by bombing raids
- they could afford black market goods
- they had goods or skills that they could trade for things they needed.

People did badly if:

- they were a group the government did not help – Jewish people, for example, were always given less rations and were very soon only allowed to claim potatoes out of all the foods that were rationed
- they lived in towns or cities that were bombed
- they had no family or friends to support them
- they had no useful skills and nothing valuable to trade.

Source B: From a letter written by Hermine Jundt, who lived in the town of Mannheim, to a friend who had moved to the country.

Things are awful here now, Anna. Thirteen big bombs have dropped round about us – the craters are the biggest I've ever seen, and the dirt and rubble in the house and yard is worse than ever. The only clean place is the cellar. When we got back home I just wanted to howl. I didn't know where to begin. No lights, no water, no gas. I tried to light a fire and what a smoke came into the room! When I looked outside a piece of mattress had landed on top of the chimney!

There were 180,000 incendiary bombs dropped on the town, so you can imagine the fires were burning for hours on end. Anna, I'm afraid you won't see many of your old neighbours again.

Source C: From an interview in 1989 with Sigrid Wendt about living through the war in the town of Brunswick.

By 1944 you could hardly get anything worth having with your clothing coupons. You could undo flour sacks and sew them into underwear for the children. If the children were at school, or out playing in the street or garden, that gave mum time to try to get in something to eat. That was a time-consuming business. It meant going along to the butchers with your empty jug to see if you could get a few blood and flour sausages or a drop of offal soup. There were always queues and often the person in front of you got the last bit. If that happened then it was just a bit of bread topped with a spread we made from dried egg powder and skimmed milk.

Activities

1 In what ways did life in Germany change during the years 1939-1945?

   Write a brief essay answering this question. You may use the following in your answer:

   - Bombing
   - Shortages

   You must also include information of your own.

2 Study Source A. Write two captions for this photograph – one for a German newspaper and one for an English one.

3 Describe the ways in which housewives had to adapt during the war. Use Sources B and C and any other information you find useful.

4 In pairs, discuss how the tone of Sources B and C differ. Why do you think this is?

Summary

- Schacht's autarky policy and Göering's Four Year Plan aimed to make Germany self-sufficient.
- Rearmament, the Labour Service and 'invisible unemployment' cut unemployment 1933-1939.
- Working conditions were improved by Beauty of Labour and Strength through Joy, but Trade Unions were banned and wages and hours fixed.
- The war brought bombing, rationing and other hardships to civilians in Germany.

3.3 Nazi treatment of minorities, including the 'Final Solution'

Learning outcomes

By the end of this topic you should be able to:

- understand Nazi racial policies
- explain Nazi policies towards minorities including the Jews
- describe the 'Final Solution'.

Anti-Semitism: Opposition to, and attack on, Jews

Final Solution: The Nazi policy to exterminate all Jews in Europe

Ghetto: An area of a city or town used for one racial group

Untermenschen: German word for 'sub-humans', including Jews and Slavs

Getting an overview

The Nazis were determined to create a master race of Aryans – tall, fair-haired and blue-eyed. This would be achieved through selective breeding. At the same time, Hitler was determined to eliminate what he saw as inferior races, such as the Jews.

Activities

1 Identify two things you can learn from Source A about Nazi views of the Jews.

2 Find three examples of how the treatment of Jews got worse from 1933–1939.

Source A: An illustration from a children's textbook. It shows Jewish people leaving Germany. The sign reads 'One way street'.

Nazi racial views

Central to Nazi policy was the creation of a pure German state. The Nazis divided the different races into two groups: the *Herrenvolk*, or master race, and the *Untermenschen*, 'sub-humans'.

The 'master race'

The Nazis believed that the Germans were of pure Aryan descent, from the *Herrenvolk* or 'master race'. They were depicted as being very Scandinavian looking – tall, blue-eyed, blond-haired and athletic.

Source A: Profile of the ideal Aryan male, who is hard-working.

Source B: From a speech by Heinrich Himmler, Head of the SS, in 1935.

'The first principle for us was and is the recognition of the values of blood and selection. We sorted out the people whom we thought unsuitable for the formation of the SS simply on the basis of outward appearances.'

Hitler wanted to create a master race through selective breeding. The SS were central to the drive for selective breeding and only recruited men who were of Aryan blood. In other words, they were tall, fair-haired and blue-eyed. They could only marry women of pure Aryan blood. Indeed, there were race farms all over Germany to breed Aryan children. Here, members of the SS and women of pure Aryan stock bred the pure Aryan master race of the future.

Source C: From the Nazi weekly magazine *Racial Research*.

'We demand of a member of this noble race that he marry only a blue-eyed, oval-faced, red-cheeked and thin-nosed blonde woman. We demand that he take a wife, a virgin only. We demand that the blue-eyed Aryan hero marry an Aryan girl who like himself is of pure and unblemished past.'

The *Untermenschen*

Other races, especially Jews and Slavs (people from Eastern Europe), were seen as inferior or sub-humans. Nazi policy was that they should be removed in case they prevent the creation of the pure Aryan master race.

Hitler had used the Jews as the scapegoat for Germany's problems after 1918: the 'stab in the back' theory, the humiliating Treaty of Versailles, and the hyperinflation of 1923. There were only half a million Jews in Germany in 1933, fewer than one person in every hundred. However, they did make up 16 per cent of all lawyers and 10 per cent of all doctors. Many Germans were jealous of their success and suspicious of their very different religion. This made it easy to convince them to accept anti-Semitic policies.

Activities

1   What can you learn from Source C about Nazi views on race?
2   For what reasons did the Nazis persecute the Jews?

Treatment of minorities

The Nazis wanted Germans who could contribute to society through work, military service or motherhood. Everyone else was seen as a 'burden on the community'. This included the severely disabled, mentally ill, and unhealthy. They were not only worthless to society, but expensive to look after. Others, such as vagrants and gypsies, were seen as undesirables and a bad influence.

Activities

1 To what extent were Nazi policies towards minority groups such as gypsies, vagrants and the mentally ill determined by their views on race?

2 Explain why gypsies, vagrants and the work-shy were persecuted by the Nazis.

Gypsies

Gypsies were seen as a real threat because they held a strong group identity and refused to conform to Nazi ideals. They were non-Aryan and thought to be work-shy. Although there were only 30,000 in Germany, the Nazis were determined to prevent them from mixing with Aryans. In 1935, marriages between gypsies and Aryans were banned. In 1938, a decree for the 'Struggle against the Gypsy Plague' was issued. This forced gypsies to register so they could be controlled.

Source A: Dr Ritter, head of the Nazi Institute of Criminal Biology.

'The gypsy question can be considered solved only when the majority of the asocial and unproductive gypsies are placed in large work camps and the further reproduction of this half-caste population is terminated.'

Vagrants

Vagrants included beggars, men moving from town to town trying to find work and young people who had left home. The Nazis forced these groups to work. In 1938 the SS rounded up c.11,000 vagrants and placed them in concentration camps.

Source B: SS Officer Greifelt in January 1939.

'In view of the tight situation on the labour market, national labour discipline dictated that all persons who would not conform to the working life of the nation, and who were vegetating as work-shy and asocial, making the streets of our cities and countryside unsafe, had to be compulsorily registered and set to work. More than 10,000 of these asocial forces are currently undertaking a labour training cure in the concentration camps.'

Treatment of minorities

Black people

Black people were seen as *Untermenschen* too. The Nuremberg Laws of 1935 banned marriage between German Aryans and black people. The Nazis treated black people in much the same way as gypsies. Indeed they sterilized any children who were born to German women by black soldiers who had been stationed in the Rhineland after the First World War.

Mentally ill and disabled

The Nazis did not want mentally ill or disabled people in the Nazi state, even if they came from 'good' German families. At first, they simply sterilized the mentally ill, so they could not have children. Then, from August 1939, the Nazis began to encourage people to send disabled and mentally ill relatives to state run clinics for 'special care'. These people had their rations slowly reduced until they starved to death, or were left exposed in cold weather to freeze. In the autumn of 1939, the Nazis began the T4 programme, the systematic gassing of the mentally ill, disabled and people with hereditary diseases. Over 70,000 people, many of them children, were killed in six different centres. But, in 1941, due to news of the centres leaking out, the Nazis had to stop T4. This didn't mean they stopped killing – the Nazis set up more secret centres and carried on gassing. In all, between August 1938 and the end of the war in 1945, over 200,000 mentally ill and disabled people were killed.

Treatment of Jews, 1933–1939

The Nazis were determined to force the Jews to leave Germany through a policy of persecution.

Anti-Jewish propaganda

The cinema, posters, newspapers and even school textbooks were all used to portray the Jews as evil moneylenders who were not to be trusted.

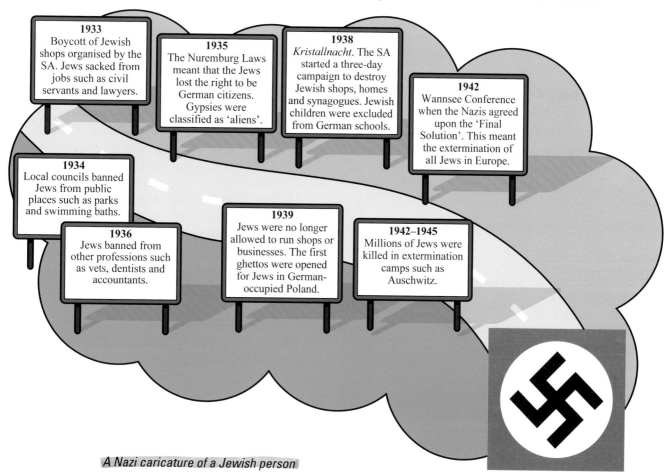

1933
Boycott of Jewish shops organised by the SA. Jews sacked from jobs such as civil servants and lawyers.

1935
The Nuremburg Laws meant that the Jews lost the right to be German citizens. Gypsies were classified as 'aliens'.

1938
Kristallnacht. The SA started a three-day campaign to destroy Jewish shops, homes and synagogues. Jewish children were excluded from German schools.

1942
Wannsee Conference when the Nazis agreed upon the 'Final Solution'. This meant the extermination of all Jews in Europe.

1934
Local councils banned Jews from public places such as parks and swimming baths.

1936
Jews banned from other professions such as vets, dentists and accountants.

1939
Jews were no longer allowed to run shops or businesses. The first ghettos were opened for Jews in German-occupied Poland.

1942–1945
Millions of Jews were killed in extermination camps such as Auschwitz.

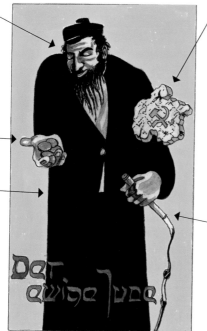

A Nazi caricature of a Jewish person

Jews portrayed as evil-looking with particularly large noses

Reference to the wealth of Jews. Many Germans were resentful of Jews who were well off

To show the different customs of dress so Germans would regard them as outsiders or aliens

The Nazis encouraged Germans to believe that the Jews were close allies of international communism. This encouraged big business to support the Nazis and turn against Jewish businesses

To create an image of cruelty and savagery

Source A: From a history textbook used in a German school in 1942.

The Jewish race is much inferior to the Negro race.

All Jews have crooked legs, fat bellies, curly hair and look untrustworthy.

The Jews were responsible for the First World War.

They are to blame for the armistice of 1918 and the Versailles Treaty.

They caused the inflation of 1923.

They brought about the downfall of the Roman Empire.

Karl Marx is a great criminal.

All Jews are communists.

They are rulers of Russia.

Activities

1 Give three examples of how propaganda made many Germans turn against the Jews.
2 Study Source A on page 97. Identify for which past events the Jews are blamed.

Attacks on property

Within a few months of becoming Chancellor in March 1933 Hitler ordered the SA to turn customers away from Jewish shops marking a new phase in Nazi policy. They also smashed windows in some Jewish shops and painted '*Jude*' (Jew) on doors and windows. This boycott was extended to Jewish lawyers and doctors all over Germany.

Source B: Official statement from the Nazi Party, 30 March 1933.

'Boycott Committees against the Jews throughout the whole Reich. On 1 April, at the stroke of ten, the boycott of all Jewish businesses, doctors, lawyers begins – ten thousand mass gatherings. The Jews have declared war on 65 millions, now they are to be hit where it hurts them most.'

Source C: SA and SS men carrying out the boycott of Jewish shops in 1933.

During the summer of 1933, placards appeared outside shops, cafes, swimming pools, parks and many other public places throughout Germany saying either 'Jews not wanted' or 'Jews forbidden'.

In 1937, the Aryanisation of Jewish businesses was stepped up. More and more Jewish businesses were confiscated. In April 1938, Jews had to register their property, thus making it easier to confiscate. Finally, in 1939, Jews were no longer allowed to run shops or businesses.

Loss of jobs

In 1933, Hitler ordered the sacking from government jobs of anyone not of Aryan descent. Thousands of Jewish civil servants were immediately sacked. Nazi school authorities sacked Jewish teachers. Jewish actors and musicians were forbidden to perform in public. In 1935, Jews were forbidden to join the army.

In 1936, the professional activities of Jews were banned or restricted. This included vets, dentists, accountants, surveyors, teachers and nurses. Two years later, Jewish doctors, dentists and lawyers were forbidden to treat or work for Aryans and effectively they could only deal with Jewish people.

Loss of social position

The social position of Jews was also systematically undermined by the Nazis. In 1934, local councils banned Jews from public places such as parks, playing fields and swimming pools. In 1938, Jewish children were excluded from German schools and universities. Jews with non-Jewish first names had to add and use the name 'Israel' for males and 'Sarah' for females. They also had to have the red letter 'J' stamped on their passports.

In the same year, Jews were banned from all theatres, shows, concert and lecture halls, museums, amusement places and sports fields. In the following year, they were no longer allowed to own radios or to buy cakes and chocolate. The 1941 decree ordering them to wear Stars of David made of yellow cloth further degraded the position of Jews by clearly marking them out in society.

The Nuremberg Laws

The Nuremberg Laws were passed in 1935 and denied Jews the basic right of German citizenship, marking the start of a new phase in Nazi policy. The *Reich* Citizenship Law made Jews 'subjects' rather than citizens. In other words, the Jews lost the right to vote and to hold government office. The Law for the Protection of German Blood and Honour banned marriages between Jews and Aryans and forbade any sexual relations outside marriage.

Source D: A caricature of a Jew with the words 'Jews not welcome'. This was placed at the entrance to a beer hall.

Kristallnacht

The most violent actions taken against the Jews in the years 1933–1939 occurred on 9–10 November 1938. This followed the murder of Ernst vom Rath, a secretary in the German embassy in Paris, by Herschel Grynspan, a Polish Jew. At a reunion of those involved in the Munich *Putsch*, Goebbels seized on this event as an excuse to suggest a campaign of terror against the Jews. Hitler agreed.

Source E: Instructions from the Reich Central Bureau for Security, November 1938.

'Only such measures may be employed as will not endanger German lives or property – for example, synagogues may only be burnt when there is no risk that fire will spread to neighbouring structures. Jewish stores and dwellings may be destroyed but not plundered. The police must not interfere with the demonstrations that will occur. Only as many Jews – particularly wealthy ones – should be arrested as can be accommodated in available jails.'

This led to *Kristallnacht* (Night of Broken Glass), 9–10 November 1938, so called because of the thousands of Jewish shop windows that were smashed, with over 815 shops destroyed, 191 synagogues set on fire and 76 synagogues demolished. Additionally, 91 Jews were killed and a further 20,000 arrested.

Many Germans watched the events of *Kristallnacht* with alarm and concern. However, the Nazi-controlled press presented it as a spontaneous reaction of ordinary Germans against Jews. Most Germans did not believe this, but hardly anyone protested for fear of arrest and death.

To make matters worse, Göring required Jews to meet the cost of damage to their property themselves. On 12 November 1938, the Jewish community was ordered to pay a fine of 1 billion *reichsmarks*. On the same day, a decree was issued barring Jews from owning or managing businesses.

Activities

3 Working in pairs, make a copy of the following table.

	Rating 1–10	Explanation
Property		
Jobs		
Social position		
Nuremberg Laws		

a) Give each area of Jewish persecution a score of 1 to 10 to indicate how serious it was in affecting the position of Jews (1 = not serious at all, 10 = very serious).

b) Give a brief explanation of each choice.

4 Explain the importance of the Nuremberg Laws for the position of the Jews in Germany.

5 In what ways did the position of German Jews change in the years 1933–1938?

6 Was *Kristallnacht* due to popular German anti-Semitism? Explain your answer.

The 'Final Solution'

Shortly before the outbreak of the Second World War, the persecution of the Jews in Germany had intensified. In January 1939, the *Reich* Central Office for Jewish Emigration was set up with Reinhard Heydrich as its director. The aim was forced emigration of German Jews. However, at this stage, the Nazis did not seem to have considered the mass slaughter of Jews.

The outbreak of war changed Nazi attitudes to the Jewish question in three ways.

1. It allowed a more extreme treatment of the Jews without concern for world opinion.
2. Early German successes increased the number of Jews under Nazi control and removed the very areas they had hoped to use for forced emigration.
3. Finally, it meant that the Nazis had to come up with more extreme solutions, especially because of the 3 million Jews in German-occupied west Poland.

Ghettos

Ghettos were the first solution. The Nazis gathered all the Jews into ghettos or 'Jewish reservations' in towns. Walls were built to keep them in. The largest ghetto was in Warsaw. The Germans allowed only starvation rations in to the ghettos, and thousands died from hunger, the intense cold or the disease typhus. Almost 100,000 died in the Warsaw ghetto.

Source A: A survivor remembers her first days in the Vilna ghetto in Poland.

'As we entered, we were directed to a house that would have been occupied by a family of four to six people under normal conditions. Now 25 to 30 of us were crammed in. Everybody was searching for a place to sleep. I was lucky. My mother found an empty space under a table and that became my bed. Going to the synagogue, praying and studying about our religion were absolutely forbidden. The Germans wanted to break the Jewish spirit and morale. Many people lost their will to live, but I was too stubborn to give in.'

Einsatzgruppen

In June 1941, the Germans invaded Russia. The Nazis organised special murder squads known as the *Einsatzgruppen*, who moved into Russia behind the advancing German armies with the express purpose of rounding up and killing Jews. They raided towns and villages and picked out any Jews, who were then marched to the outskirts of villages, forced to dig their own graves, and then shot. By 1943, it is estimated that the *Einsatzgruppen* had murdered over 2 million Russians, mainly Jews.

Source B: Women and girls from Dvinsk about to be shot by the *Einsatzgruppen*.

Activities

1. Give an example of one change in Nazi policy towards Jews after the outbreak of the Second World War.
2. Study Source A. Give two examples of the harsh treatment of Jews in ghettos.

Wannsee Conference

In the summer of 1941, a decision was taken by senior Nazi leaders to seek a permanent and final solution to the Jewish question. It was to exterminate them in death camps. Although Göring signed the order, it seems to have been mainly the idea of Himmler as a means of dealing with the problem of the increasing number of Jews in German-occupied areas.

Source C: Höss, the Commandant of Auschwitz, from his autobiography written in 1945.

'In the summer of 1941, I cannot remember the exact date, Himmler received me and said in effect: "The *Führer* has ordered that the Jewish question be solved once and for all. The Jews are the sworn enemies of the German people and must be eradicated. Every Jew that we can lay our hands on is to be destroyed now during the war, without exception. If we cannot obliterate the biological basis of Jewry, the Jews will one day destroy the German people."'

In January 1942, leading Nazis met at Wannsee in Berlin to work out the details of the '**Final Solution**'. Death camps were built in Poland, far away from Germany, where Jews were to be worked to death. Work on building gas chambers and crematoria at camps was accelerated. The first camp began operating on 17 March 1942 at Belzec on the eastern Polish border. By the summer of 1943, Jews from all over Europe were being transported to these camps.

The death camps

On arrival at the death camps, the Jews were divided into two groups. Those who were fit were put to work. The others were sent to the gas chambers. However, those who were put to work were not much better off: they were worked to death in the labour camps.

Older women, mothers with small children, pregnant women and children under 10 were usually taken away immediately to be executed. Young boys would lie about their age and invent a skill or craft in order to be given work and stay alive.

Source D: Camps in Germany and Poland.

Source E: Errikos Sevillias describes his arrival at Auschwitz.

'As we huddled together, the SS quickly separated the men from the women. They took the old and the sick and put them in a special line… The doctor who examined me held my arm down on a table and tattooed it with the number 182699. My entire body was shaved, then I was given a shower and afterwards issued with clothes which had huge red painted marks on them. This was so I could be easily spotted if I tried to escape.'

Many died in the gas chambers from carbon monoxide and Zyclon B gasses. The Nazi aim was to carry out the 'Final Solution' as efficiently as possible. For example at Treblinka, 140,000 were killed each month in 1942. Most gas chambers were fitted out as showers so that the prisoners would not realise what was happening to them. Bodies were burnt in ovens or left in mass pits.

Source F: Höss, the Commandant of Auschwitz, from his autobiography written in 1945.

'I had to watch coldly while mothers with laughing or crying children went into the gas chamber. I had to see everything. I had to watch hour by hour, by night by day, the burning and the removal of the bodies, the extraction of the teeth, the cutting of the hair, the whole grisly business. In the face of such grim considerations I was forced to bury all human feelings as deeply as possible.'

Activities

3 Study Sources E and G. What do they suggest about life in an extermination camp?

4 Study Source F. What justification does Höss give for his actions?

5 Why did the Nazis decide on the Final Solution?

Source G: Roll call at Auschwitz-Birkenau drawn by a prisoner, Ella Liebermann.

Prisoners who were not gassed were given various jobs to do, the worst being the removal of the dead bodies from the gas chambers. There was a strict daily routine, with roll calls for several hours per day before forced labour in mines or factories. The conditions were terrible. Food, which consisted of bread and thin soup, was very scarce. Diseases spread quickly. In addition, some inmates were used for medical experiments – generally without anaesthetics. (Doctors were experimenting to create the perfect Aryan type.)

By the time the camps were liberated by the Allies in 1945, 6 million Jews and 500,000 European gypsies, as well as countless other prisoners, had been worked to death, gassed or shot.

Source H: A German policeman testifying in 1961.

'I believed the propaganda that all Jews were criminals and sub-humans and that they were the cause of Germany's decline after the First World War. The thought that one should disobey or evade the order to participate in the extermination of the Jews did not therefore enter my mind at all.'

Source I: From a school history textbook, written in 1997.

'There was little German opposition to these aspects of the Nazis' work because Hitler had been so effective in removing all opposition within Germany and placing Nazis in positions of power. Germans were subjected to a constant barrage of anti-Semitic propaganda. Some believed it. Of some things, Germans were simply not told. For many ordinary Germans who felt powerless to resist the persecution of the Jews, they consoled themselves with the thought that this was the price they had to pay for all the "benefits" of Hitler's rule.'

Activities

6 Why do you think there is no direct evidence of when the decision to carry out the 'Final Solution' was taken?

7 In what ways did the Nazi treatment of the Jews change in the years 1939–1945? You may use the following in your answer and any other information of your own:

- Ghettos
- *Einsatzgruppen*
- 'Final Solution'.

8 'The German people were responsible for the "Final Solution".' Discuss.

 examzone **Watch out!**

It is important not to focus only on Nazi treatment of the Jews, unless the question specifically asks you to do so. To explain Nazi policies and ideology you need to mention all the types of people that were seen as inferior to the Nazi ideal.

Summary

- The Nazi theory of race was to create an Aryan master race and to remove the *Untermenschen* or sub-humans, such as the Jews.
- The Nazis were determined to remove anybody who was not of use to the regime. This included gypsies and the mentally ill.
- Hitler gradually introduced a series of measures aimed at forcing Jews to leave Germany. These included the Nuremberg Laws of 1935 and *Kristallnacht*.
- The outbreak of the Second World War meant that the Nazis had to change their policies towards the Jews from ghettos, to murder squads, to the 'Final Solution', carried out in specially built extermination camps.

1933
Boycott of Jewish shops

1934
Jews banned from public places

1935
Gypsies classified as aliens. Nuremberg Laws

1938
Kristallnacht Jewish businesses taken over by the Nazis

1939
Setting up of ghettos for Jews

1941
Setting up of *Einsatzgruppen*

1942
Wannsee Conference and 'Final Solution'

1942–1945
Use of extermination camps to gas Jews

1945
Liberation of camps by Allies

Quick quiz

1 How good is your knowledge of German terms? What do the following terms mean?

Deutsches Jungvolk

Jung Mädel

Autobahns

Autarky

Schönheit der Arbeit

Kraft durch Freude

2 In each row a)–g) in the following table, identify which term is the odd one out. Explain your choice.

			Odd one out	Reason
a) Jews	Gypsies	Germans		
b) Jews lose jobs	Labour Service	Invisible unemployment		
c) Race studies	Maths	Eugenics		
d) *Untermenschen*	Blond	Aryan race		
e) League of German maidens	Hitler Youth	Physical education		
f) Boys	Military drill	History		
g) Education	Three 'K's'	Women		

3. Identify which of the following statements is a cause, an event or an effect. Organise them in the following table to describe their historical sequence.

a) A Nazi official in Paris was murdered by a Jew.

b) The SS organised the systematic destruction of shops and the burning of synagogues.

c) Children were indoctrinated with Nazi ideas.

d) In 1935 the Nuremberg Laws were passed.

e) The Jews were denied German citizenship.

f) Göring forced the Jews to pay a fine for the damage caused by *Kristallnacht*.

g) Hitler wanted to control the lives of young people.

h) Teachers had to be members of the Nazi Party.

i) Hitler blamed the Jews for the German defeat in the First World War and the subsequent economic crises.

Causes	Events	Effects

Checklist

How well do you know and understand the following topics?

- ◑ Nazi policies towards women.
- ◑ The successes and failures of these policies.
- ◑ Nazi policies towards the young.
- ◑ Nazi attempts to reduce unemployment.
- ◑ The Nazi economic policies.
- ◑ The standard of living under the Nazis.
- ◑ Nazi racial policies.
- ◑ Nazi policies towards minorities including the Jews.
- ◑ The 'Final Solution'.

Student tip

You will improve your answers by including precise knowledge and details of events, which could include statistics, names and dates. For example, candidates often give generalised statements about the fall in unemployment, such as 'Hitler managed to get rid of unemployment in Germany'. More precise knowledge would be 'Unemployment in Germany fell from 6 million in 1933 to about 300,000 in 1939'.

Plenary activities

Work in small groups. Imagine it is 1933 and you work at the Nazi Ministry of Education. What changes will you make to the following school timetable and extract from a history textbook?

School timetable for girls

Lessons	1	2	3	4	5
Subject	German	Science	Maths	History	Domestic Science

School timetable for boys

Lessons	1	2	3	4	5
Subject	Maths	History	Science	German	Geography

An extract from a history textbook written before the Nazis came to power.

In November 1918 the Republic had no choice but to agree to the armistice. In January 1919, Germany had its first democratic republic, which gave the German people much freedom and many rights. The Weimar Republic then had no choice but to sign the Treaty of Versailles and had to make crippling reparations payments. These payments led to the hyperinflation of 1923. In the same year an extreme party, the Nazis, led by a strange individual called Adolf Hitler, failed miserably in its attempt to seize power in Munich. Hitler actually ran away from the gun battle between his supporters and the police.

The key to success in exams and revision often lies in good planning. Knowing **what** you need to do and **when** you need to do it is your best path to a stress-free experience. Here are some top tips in creating a great personal revision plan.

First of all, **know your strengths and weaknesses**.

Go through each topic making a list of how well you think you know the topic. Use your mock examination results and/or any other test results that are available as a check on your self-assessment. This will help you to plan your personal revision effectively, putting extra time into your weaker areas.

Next, *create your plan!*

Remember to make time for considering how topics interrelate.

For example, in History you will be expected to know not just what happened, but why it happened, how important it was and how one event relates to another.

The specification quite clearly states when you are expected to be able to link one topic to another so plan this into your revision sessions.

You will be tested on this in the exam and you can do well by showing your ability to do this.

Finally, *follow the plan!*

You can use the revision sections in the following pages to kick-start your revision.

MAY

SUNDAY	MONDAY	TU
29	30	1

Be realistic about how much time you can devote to your revision, but also make sure you put in enough time. Give yourself regular breaks or different activities to give your life some variety. Revision need not be a prison sentence!

Find out your exam dates. Go to the Edexcel website to find all final exam dates, and check with your teacher.

iew Se
omplet
ractice
quest

Chunk your revision in each subject down into smaller sections. This will make it more manageable and less daunting.

Draw up a list of all the dates from the start of your revision right through to your exams.

13

Review Sectio
Complete three
practice exam

20

Review Sectio
Try the Keywor
Quiz again

Make sure you allow time for assessing your progress against your initial self-assessment. Measuring progress will allow you to see and be encouraged by your improvement. These little victories will build your confidence.

22

EXAM DAY!

27

28

29

Mini exam paper

1 Study Source A.

Source A: A photograph of a Hitler Youth rally at Nuremberg in 1933.

What can you learn from Source A about the appeal of the Nazi Party in the 1930s. (4 marks)

2 The boxes below show two groups.

Choose **one** and explain the importance of that group's work for the success of the Nazi Party. (9 marks)

The SA 1923–1934 (Brownshirts)	The SS 1934–1945

Answer **EITHER** Question 3 **OR** Question 4.

EITHER

3 Why was the Weimar Republic unpopular in the years 1919–1923? (12 marks)

> You may use the following in your answer.
> - The terms of the Treaty of Versailles
> - Hyperinflation
>
> You must also include information of your own.

This question is only worth 4 marks. This means that you should spend no more than 6 minutes on it – do not waste time that you might need later by going into too much detail! Two sentences are all you need to write.

You will always be given a choice for question 2.

Note the key words in this question (importance and success) and the years. You will not get any credit for information you give that refers to events outside the span of years given.

You will always be given a source in Question 1. Make sure you study it carefully as you will need to use it to answer the question. Whatever you mention must be in the source and **not** just come from your own knowledge.

It is really important that you DO NOT just write everything you know about one of these. You need to concentrate on what the question asks you – underline the key word in the question – in this case you need to explain what the group contributed to Nazi success.

This information is here to help you! This means that these two points will be relevant to the question. You do not have to use any of the bullet points, and you will not lose marks for leaving any of them out, but you should mention them if you can. It does not mean that is all you need to write though – if you can think of other reasons then add those too!

These questions are worth 12 marks so it is important that you spend more time on them (about 18 minutes). You might want to jot a few ideas down before you write.

OR

4 Why was the Weimar Republic able to survive in the years 1924–1929? (12 marks)

You may use the following in your answer.
- A new currency
- Loans from the USA

You must also include information of your own.

These directions are important. Make sure that you read all four questions **and** that you can answer both parts of the question before you make your choice. Remember that question part (b) carries the most marks.

Answer **EITHER** Question 5 **OR** Question 6.

You must answer both parts of the question you choose.

Spelling, punctuation and grammar will be assessed in *(b)

EITHER

Pick out the key words in the questions. In this case they are **describe the ways** and **able to win support from different groups**. Many students lose marks because they do not read the questions properly.

5 (a) Describe the ways in which the Nazi Party was able to win support from different groups in Germany in the years 1929–1932. (9 marks)

***(b)** Why was Hitler able to gain complete power in governing Germany in the years 1933–1934? Explain your answer. (16 marks)

You may use the following in your answer.
- The *Reichstag* fire
- The death of President Hindenburg

You must also include information of your own.

This information is here to help you! This means that these two pieces of information will be relevant to the question. You do not have to use them, and you will not lose marks for leaving them out, but you should mention them if you can. Remember that you must use information of your own if you want to get high marks.

Again, this information is here for a reason – to help you! Do not ignore it. You must also use information of your own if you want to get high marks. Remember, too, that this is a *(b) question and the examiners will be able to give you up to four marks for correct spelling, punctuation and grammar.

OR

6 (a) Describe the role played by women in the Nazi state in the years 1933–1945. (9 marks)

***(b)** In what ways did the Nazi treatment of Jews change in the years 1933–1945? Explain your answer. (16 marks)

You may use the following in your answer.
- The Nuremberg Laws
- The death camps

You must also include information of your own.

Take note of the years in **all** questions. Any information you write that is outside the period will not gain you any marks.

The full versions of these questions are shown on pages 107 and 108.

1 What can you learn from Source A about the appeal of the Nazi Party in the 1930s? (4 marks)

Student answer	Comments	Improved student answer
The Nazi Party must have had lots of members.	The candidate offers a simple inference, but does not relate it to the question or the source, or explain its relevance. To improve, the answer needs to make an inference from the source about the appeal of the Nazi Party and explain how they made the inference.	This is a Hitler Youth march. The Nazi Party wanted to extend its appeal across young people as well as adults and this photo suggests it had a lot of success. The uniforms, the banners and the sense of belonging to a powerful, supportive group probably appealed to many young men.
They are in uniforms and carrying banners.	The candidate extracts information from the source but does not relate it to the question or explain its relevance. To improve, the answer needs to make an inference from the source about the appeal of the Nazi Party and explain how they made the inference.	This is a Hitler Youth march. Many young people joined the Hitler Youth. It gave them a sense of belonging and security. They got a lot of encouragement and praise for their membership and the source shows how they are marching as a unit, with uniforms and banners.

2 Explain the importance of the SA's work for the success of the Nazi Party. (9 marks)

Student answer	Comments	Improved student answer
The SA were Hitler's private army. He needed them to come to power. They bullied his political opponents and kept some members out of the Reichstag for the votes after the fire.	The candidate has discussed what their chosen group did, but has not explained how that helped the Nazi Party succeed. To improve the answer, the candidate needs to focus on the significance of the group to the success of the Nazi Party.	The SA were Hitler's private army. They broke up the meetings of his opponents in the early years, making other opposition groups (such as the communists) look weaker at a point when voters wanted a strong party. Also, they stopped some deputies going into the Reichstag to vote after the Reichstag Fire, and this was vital to him getting the Enabling Act passed.

3 Why was the Weimar republic unpopular in the years 1919-1923? (12 marks)
You may use the following in your answer.
- The terms of the Treaty of Versailles
- Hyperinflation
You must also include information of your own.

Student answer	Comments	Improved student answer
The Weimar Republic was unpopular because of the Treaty of Versailles. The Germans had the treaty imposed on them and had to accept war guilt and pay high reparations.	The candidate has chosen one reason for the unpopularity of the Weimar Republic and given detail to support it, but has not explained why the Treaty made the Weimar Republic unpopular. Also, the question gives two points to consider and asks for extra information, which has not been given.	The Weimar Republic was unpopular because it signed the Treaty of Versailles. The German people resented the treaty because they felt it was unfair – especially that Germany had the treaty imposed on them (the Diktat) and had to accept war guilt and pay high reparations. Also, the Republic wasn't dealing with the very severe inflation where people were having a hard time because money was worthless. Another thing to consider is how it made itself unpopular by allowing right- and left-wing political parties to exist and criticise it.
The Weimar Republic was unpopular for many reasons. The Treaty of Versailles was very unpopular with the German people. Hyperinflation was making them suffer, too.	The candidate has mentioned both suggested points but has not given any detail about how or why they made the Weimar Republic unpopular. The question gives two points to consider and asks for extra information which has not been given.	The Weimar Republic was unpopular for many reasons. Firstly, because it signed the Treaty of Versailles. This treaty was imposed on them (the 'Diktat'), which the German people didn't think was fair. They also resented that they had to accept war guilt and pay high reparations. Secondly, the Republic wasn't dealing with hyperinflation. People were desperate for the government to act decisively to stop this. Thirdly, it was getting a lot of criticism from right- and left-wing parties, and wasn't dealing with that, either.
The Weimar Republic was unpopular for many reasons. It signed the Treaty of Versailles, which the German people thought was an unfair treaty.	The candidate has explained their reasons and covered both points. They have used their own information to explain the reasons, but have not provided additional reasons beyond the two points in the question.	The Weimar Republic was unpopular for many reasons. Firstly, because it signed the Treaty of Versailles – they were so resented for this that those who signed were called the 'November Criminals'. The treaty (called the 'Diktat') was imposed on Germany – it was humiliating not even to be asked to the negotiations. Most Germans also resented the 'war guilt' clause where Germany had to take responsibility for starting the war – no nation had had to do that before.

They resented that Germany had not been at the negotiations, that they had to accept the 'war guilt' clause and that they had to pay high reparations. Secondly, the Republic wasn't dealing with hyperinflation. People were desperate for the government to act decisively to stop this, because money wasn't worth anything.

Also, Germany lost land, couldn't have a big army and had to pay high reparations. It all seemed very unfair. Secondly, the Republic wasn't dealing with hyperinflation. People were desperate for the government to act decisively to stop this, because it was making savings, wages and pensions etc worthless. Many different groups in Germany, from factory owners to pensioners to workers, were struggling to make do. Thirdly, the Republic was getting a lot of criticism from right- and left-wing parties because it allowed free speech. This meant that people were hearing criticism from these parties on all sides. While they disagreed wildly over the reforms the government should be making, they all agreed it wasn't acting firmly enough or fast enough.

5 a) Describe the ways in which the Nazi Party was able to win support from different groups in Germany in the years 1929-32. (9 marks)

Student answer	Comments	Improved student answer
They got support by the clever use of propaganda.	The candidate has suggested a valid reason for the growth of support for the Nazis, but has not explained or given examples.	The Nazis got support by clever use of propaganda, organised by Goebbels. They had posters with simple strong slogans about providing work or bread. They targeted different groups (e.g. women and workers) with different slogans.
They got support by the clever use of propaganda and because the Wall Street Crash and the Depression in the USA had a big effect on Germany. The USA stopped lending Germany money, and even wanted money paid back. Lots of German businesses were only keeping going because of these loans, so they failed. So there was unemployment and a depression in Germany that the Weimar Republic couldn't fix, so people looked for a strong party to support.	The candidate has suggested valid reasons for the growth of support and has described one. To improve, the answer needs to explain how the reason(s) led to support for the Nazis.	The Nazis got support by the clever use of propaganda and because the Depression in the USA that followed the Wall Street Crash meant the USA stopped lending Germany money, and even wanted money paid back. Lots of German businesses that were relying on the loans collapsed. So there was unemployment and a depression in Germany. The Weimar Republic could not end the depression. They were slow to act and the Nazis were quick to condemn them as weak. Nazi propaganda said the Nazis would provide things people needed (such as work) and said they would be a strong government.
They got support from different people for different reasons. They were careful to show themselves as strong (and most people wanted a strong government) and then they targeted different people with different messages.	This is the framework of a good answer, but needs detail to explain the points the candidate is making.	They got support from different people for different reasons. They were careful to show themselves as strong (and most people wanted a strong government) with their almost military discipline. They also suggested that, as well as the Weimar government, there were other groups to blame for the problems in Germany (Jews, communists and unions) that the Nazis would bring under control. Then they targeted different people with different messages – for example, they promised the unemployed work (and ran soup kitchens to show care for them). Their anti-union policies appealed to industrialists.

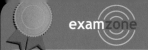
6 b) In what ways did the Nazi treatment of Jews change in the years 1933-1945? Explain your answer.
- You may use the following in your answer:
- The Nuremberg Laws
- The death camps
You must also include information of your own. (16 marks)

Student answer	Comments	Improved student answer
The Nuremberg Laws stopped Jews doing things, like being a German citizen or marrying a non-Jew.	The candidate has chosen one change and given detail to support it, but has not explained how it was a change. Also, the question gives two points to consider and asks for extra information, which has not been given.	The Nazis began by boycotting Jewish shops in 1933. The Nuremberg Laws changed how Jews were treated by limiting Jewish rights and deprived them of German citizenship. The death camps went further and murdered them.
The Nuremberg Laws and the death camps were both changes that affected the status of Jewish people in German society.	The candidate has mentioned both suggested points, but without any detail about how or why they were changes in the treatment of Jews The question asks for extra information which has not been given.	... The Nuremberg Laws stopped Jews being German citizens and restricted other rights (e.g. who they could marry). More restrictions followed (e.g. jobs Jews could do, or places they could go - like public swimming pools). The death camps were the 'Final Solution': Jews were murdered there.
The Nazi treatment of the Jews in Germany was one of escalating isolation and violence. Anti-Semitic propaganda, shop boycotts, the Nuremberg Laws, Kristallnacht and the death camps were all moving towards getting rid of all Jews.	The candidate has thought about the focus of the question – how Nazi treatment of Jews changed and has presented it as part of an ongoing Nazi policy. It has the potential to be an excellent answer, but needs more detail to improve it.	... escalating isolation and violence. Anti-Semitic propaganda, boycotting Jewish shops (from 1933), the Nuremberg Laws (1935), Kristallnacht (1938) and the death camps (from 1942) were all part of the move towards getting rid of all Jews. The changes cut Jews off from non-Jewish neighbours and then killed them. Make sure you write accurately – there are four extra marks available for spelling, grammar and punctuation in these questions.

As you get close to completing your revision, the Big Day will be getting nearer and nearer. Many students find this the most stressful time and tend to go into panic mode, either working long hours without really giving their brains a chance to absorb information or giving up and staring blankly at the wall.

Panicking simply makes your brain seize up and you find that information and thoughts simply cannot flow naturally. You become distracted and anxious, and things seem worse than they are. Many students build the exams up into more than they are. Remember: the exams are not trying to catch you out! If you have studied the course, there will be no surprises on the exam paper!

You will have 1 hour and 15 minutes for this exam paper and in that time you have to answer four questions. You must answer questions 1 and 2 and then you have a choice between question 3 or 4, and then another choice between 5 or 6.

Each question is worth a different number of marks and it is important that you use your time effectively – don't waste precious time on question 1, which is worth only 4 marks, as that might leave you with not very much time to spend on question 5b or 6b (depending on your choice), which is worth 16 marks!

Remember too that question 5b/6b has 4 additional marks for spelling, punctuation and grammar. You need to leave enough time to write as accurately as you can and to check your writing at the end.

Student tip

I know how silly it is to panic, especially if you've done the work and know your stuff. I was asked by a teacher to produce a report on a project I'd done, and I panicked so much I spent the whole afternoon crying and worrying. I asked other people for help, but they were panicking too. In the end, I calmed down and looked at the task again. It turned out to be quite straightforward and, in the end, I got my report finished first and it was the best of them all!

In the exam you don't have much time, so you can't waste it by panicking. The best way to control panic is simply to do what you have to do. Think carefully for a few minutes, then start writing and as you do, the panic will drain away.

Don't panic

Meet the exam paper

This diagram shows the front cover of the exam paper. These instructions, information and advice will always appear on the front of the paper. It is worth reading it carefully now. Check you understand it. Now is a good opportunity to ask your teacher about anything you are not sure of here.

Print your surname here, and your other names afterwards. This is an additional safeguard to ensure that the exam board awards the marks to the right candidate.

Here you fill in the school's exam number.

Ensure that you understand exactly how long the examination will last, and plan your time accordingly.

Note that your spelling, punctuation and grammar will be assessed, and the quality of your written communication will also be marked. Take particular care to present your thoughts and work at the highest standard you can.

Here you fill in your personal exam number. Take care when writing it down because the number is important to the exam board when writing your score.

In this box, the examiner will write the total marks you have achieved in the exam paper.

Make sure that you understand exactly which questions from which sections you should attempt.

Don't feel that you have to fill the answer space provided. Everybody's handwriting varies, so a long answer from you may take up as much space a short answer from someone else.

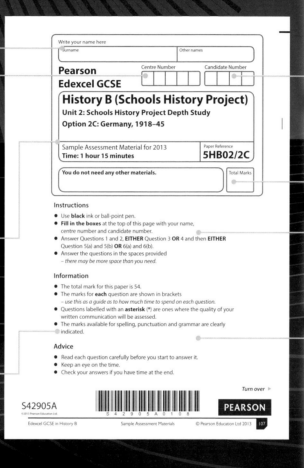

Understanding the language of the exam paper

Describe	You need to give a concise and organised account. Jot down three or four points in the margin that you want to include in your answer. Arrange them in the most logical order.
Explain how Explain why	You need to show that you understand the key events in Germany's history 1918–1945, and why they happened. The more detail you can give, the better.
Do you agree?	You are free to agree or disagree. What makes a difference is how well you back up your case and show you have considered evidence for both sides of the argument
Information of your own	You need to use information that has not been given to you in the exam paper.

Zone Out

This section provides answers to the most common questions students have about what happens after they complete their exams. For more information, visit www.examzone.co.uk

When will my results be published?

Results for GCSE examinations are issued on the third Thursday in August.

Can I get my results online?

Visit www.resultsplusdirect.co.uk, where you will find detailed student results information including the 'Edexcel Gradeometer' which demonstrates how close you were to the nearest grade boundary.

I haven't done as well as I expected. What can I do now?

First of all, talk to your teacher. After all the teaching that you have had, and the tests and internal examinations you have done, he/she is the person who best knows what grade you are capable of achieving. Take your results slip to your subject teacher, and go through the information on it in detail. If you both think that there is something wrong with the result, the school or college can apply to see your completed examination paper and then, if necessary, ask for a re-mark immediately.

Can I have a re-mark of my examination paper?

Yes, this is possible, but remember only your school or college can apply for a re-mark, not you or your parents/carers. First of all you should consider carefully whether or not to ask your school or college to make a request for a re-mark. It is worth knowing that very few re-marks result in a change to a grade – not because Ededxcel is embarrassed that a change of mark has been made, but simply because a re-mark request has shown that the original marking was accurate. Check the closing date for re-marking requests with your Examinations Officer

Bear in mind that there is no guarantee that your grades will go up if your papers are re-marked. The original mark can be confirmed or lowered, as well as raised, as a result of a re-mark.

Glossary

This Glossary contains all the key words used in the book. When appropriate the definitions are particularly directed to the period being studied.

Anti-Semitism – Opposition to, and attacks on, Jews.

Armistice – Ceasefire.

Aryan – Nazi term used to describe people of 'pure' German blood with no ancestors from races they saw as 'inferior', such as Poles, Slavs or Jews. The Nazis' ideal Aryan was white-skinned, blue-eyed, and blonde.

Autarky – Self-sufficiency.

Autobahns – German motorways.

Censorship – When unacceptable parts, or whole books, films, etc, are officially suppressed.

Coalition – A government by two or more political parties.

Concentration camps – Prisons where inmates were treated with great brutality.

Concordat – Agreement.

Conscription – Compulsory military service.

Constitution – System of rules by which a country is governed.

Democracy – Where people choose the government from two or more parties at an election.

Dictatorship – One-party state governed by one person who has total control.

Edelweiss – This flower was the symbol on the badges worn by members of the Edelweiss Pirates. It also means noble or white.

Eugenics – Study of improving the qualities of the human race.

Euthanasia – The painless killing, usually by drugs, of a patient with an incurable disease. This was practised by the Nazis on many elements of society they deemed undesirable.

Final Solution – The Nazi policy to exterminate all Jews in Europe.

Führer – German for leader.

Gestapo – Nazi secret police.

Ghetto – An area of a city or town used for one racial group.

Hyperinflation – When prices go up very quickly.

Indoctrination – Brainwashing people into accepting ideas.

Invisible unemployed – Unemployed not counted in official figures.

Judiciary – Judges.

Kaiser – German title for Emperor.

Labour exchanges – Job centres.

Lebensraum – Living space.

Orator – A fluent and effective public speaker.

Passive resistance – To resist authority in a peaceful, non-violent way.

Police state – A totalitarian state controlled by a political police force.

Propaganda – False or misleading information given out to spread certain points of view.

Proportional representation – An electoral system in which a party is given a number of representatives in direct proportion to the total number of votes for that party.

Purge – To remove enemies by terror.

Putsch – An uprising, an attempt to overthrow the government.

Real wages – Wages adjusted to allow for inflation.

Rearmament – Building up armed forces and weapons.

Reichstag – Parliament.

Reparations – Compensation for war damages paid by a defeated state.

The Ruhr – The industrial part of Germany producing coal, iron and steel.

Spartacists – The name of the German Communist Party.

The SS – The *Schutzstaffel* ('Elite Guard') were set up as Hitler's private bodyguard, and grew to control many aspects of life in the Third Reich, from the police to the economy to the death camps.

State parliament – Each German state, such as Bavaria and Saxony, elected its own parliament.

Third Reich – Third empire.

Untermenschen – German word for sub-humans, including Jews and Slavs.

Wall Street Crash – Wall Street is the home of the New York Stock Exchange. Share prices fell disastrously on Wall Street in October 1929.

Index